The Kuandaa International Handbook for Church Leaders, Volume 1

The Kuandaa International Handbook for Church Leaders,

Volume 1

Dewey Miller

RevPress

Introduction

What follows is not revolutionary. You will find no great insights. There is nothing new here. This is basic information to help leaders who want or need some fundamental guidelines for starting, leading and growing a congregation.

Although this material was originally developed with new churches in Africa in mind, the principles that it contains are true and should be universally applicable. You will hopefully find instruction, inspiration, direction, encouragement and hope as you work through this material.

The *Kuandaa International Handbook for Church Leaders, Volume 1* originally appeared as a series of articles on the kuandaa.org website. Kuandaa International is committed to working with, encouraging and training pastors throughout the world. Our work has begun in East Africa where this material was first conceived.

Ultimately, this book is intended as a resource for church leaders who are otherwise under-resourced. In fact, it is the case that many pastors in the developing world have no training or literature at all to work with. Kuandaa seeks to provide in person training events, on line resources and ongoing relationships to build up the body of Christ.

Mission

Kuandaa International is a ministry supporting the church around the world, primarily by equipping the body of Christ to do the work of ministry for the edifying of the body of Christ.

Vision

Kuandaa exists to equip church leaders around the world to minister to their congregations. Our passion is that the lost will be found, the found will be trained, and the trained will lead. The response of the pastors and leaders in East Africa has been overwhelming. The world is hungry for the Word of God and Kuandaa is trying to fill that hunger.

He… gave some to be apostles, some prophets, some evangelists, and some pastors and teachers, for the equipping of the saints for the work of ministry, for the edifying of the body of Christ… **Ephesians 4.11-12 (NKJV)**

Part One: Conversion

Repentance: First Step to Discipleship

I have written a lot about faith sharing, evangelism, church planting and the like. I do not want any of that to overshadow the actual steps to conversion. Telling someone about Jesus is not the ultimate objective in evangelism. Helping them move to faith in Christ is. So we need to spend some time thinking about how we move from evangelism prospect to fully formed and committed disciple of Jesus.

The first thing that has to happen is that an individual must come to grips with his/her sin. Christians generally think that they have a handle on this process. In fact, many people who are not a part of the faith also have the mistaken idea that they are well aware of how sin works, and how to overcome it, or at the very least they think they can minimize the effects of sin on their lives. The issues surrounding sin are deceptively simple. I think that Satan has purposely orchestrated things in such a way that humans think sin and repentance are much more complicated than they really are.

What follows then, is a short introductory course on how to overcome sin in your life.

- **Recognize your sin.** The Bible is very clear. Everyone has sin in their lives. We are all sinners. (Romans 3.10 and 3.23) The problem we have is that we often rationalize our sin, neglect our sin, or maybe we don't even notice it at all. It is essential that every thoughtful person evaluate their own lives daily. Look for where you have neglected God and his ways. Find out those places where you have violated God's law. Make it your regular practice in prayer to ask God to help you identify your sins. He will gladly illuminate your faults. Give your ego a rest and come to grips with your imperfections.

- **Repent of your sin.** This seems like a simple concept, but there is actually a lot to unpack here. First of all, repentance requires that we apologize for our wrongdoing and sin. We must tell God that we are sorry and seek to make amends with others (humans) that we have wronged. But being sorry is not enough. We must also make commitments to not sin anymore. In fact, the act of repenting carries with it the implication that you will change your life. You cannot truly be sorry unless you are committed to changing the behavior that led you to be sorry in the first place.

- **Reorient your priorities.** This is really about changing your attitudes and beliefs. To overcome sin, you have to think differently about sin. Being sorry is a beginning, but your heart will need to be changed. The things that are important to you should be the things that are important to God. Value the things and the people that God values. Spend your time and energy on positive things. Philippians 4.8 is a perfect description of orienting your priorities the things of God.

- **Re-align your actions.** Our actions are perhaps the truest indication of whether or not we have been converted. When we have repented of our sins and begun to think differently about the world, the natural result is that we will behave differently. We will do things that are in line with God's will. We will spend time with godly people in godly endeavors.

1 John 1.9 is perhaps the greatest verse in the Bible at this point. "If we confess our sins, He is faithful and just to forgive us *our* sins and to cleanse us from all unrighteousness." The good news for us is that Jesus wants to help us with our sin problem. We just need to make sure that we get through the whole process.

Assimilation: Building the Body from the Inside

A very difficult part of ministry in the local church, particularly when we are thinking about evangelism and reaching new people, is not only sharing the gospel, but getting positive responses. That is difficult to be sure, but they are not as fraught with hindrances as getting new people assimilated into the body of Christ once they are converted.

There can be no doubt that new Christians need the fellowship of other believers to support their growth in the faith. The very best place for this to happen is in the context of the local church. Specifics of how this is accomplished may vary from congregation to congregation. One church may provide an extensive system of small groups and offer spiritual accountability in that way. Others may simply offer fellowship opportunities and then consistently encourage new people to participate. No matter how your church chooses to work on assimilation, an intentional and comprehensive effort is needed.

The first steps of the assimilation process is simple.

Get In. We cannot assimilate new believers in Christ if we don't have them in our congregations. The first thing we need to do is work on a plan by which we get men and women into our church. After they are here, we will develop a three step process.

- **Identify.** Pay attention to who the new people are. Someone should always be on the lookout for visitors, first timers and the curious. Make sure that someone is keeping track of who the new people are. Once they are identified, we can begin step two.

- **Invite.** Everyone who visits should be invited to something. Ask new people to join a class, attend a small group or bake cookies for the children's ministry. Some people should be recruited to sing in the choir or help chaperone at youth events. This assumes that there are opportunities for people to be involved, and that you are open to having them involved. If that assumption is not correct, get it fixed and start over.
- **Include.** This is maybe the hardest part of assimilation. We can invite people all day, but when they come, when they begin to participate, do we make them feel wanted, valued and important? Train your people to always be on the lookout for the best way to include everyone.

Grow Up. Increasing the number of people involved in activities is not a bad thing, but it is also not the end goal of the assimilation process. We want people to get involved and participate for the sake of building disciples of Christ. To that end we specifically point individuals to events and activities that help them mature in their Christian faith. Bring people to opportunities to study the faith. Sunday school class, Bible study groups and discipleship groups are great for this purpose. As people learn about faith, while connected with others who are also on a similar journey, their commitment deepens and their faith grows.

In addition, it is good to have opportunities for new believers to serve in ministry. This was mentioned earlier, but it bears repeating here. Faith grows when we share our faith with others. Make sure that new Christians are given opportunities to serve the Lord and the church early in their faith walk.

Activities that cause individuals to work in ministry are the greatest and fastest way for faith to develop and deepen.

Go Out. Now I am just sounding like a broken record. Go out sounds like almost everything I have said previously, but it bears repeating. New people, individuals who are young in faith, become bolder, more committed and more loyal as they go out to share their faith with others.

- **Go.** There is an inherent activity required in the gospel. We must go. Unfortunately, our tendency is to want people to come to our church. We want them to meet us where we are comfortable. But Jesus asks us to go.
- **Do.** We cannot wait for someone else to make a difference in the world. We must be involved and active in the propagation of the gospel.
- **Move.** The Holy Spirit is a great partner in all of this. We must follow his leading and move with him. Just as the prophets were given the words to speak and the apostles were led where they should go, we must move with the Spirit at all times and in all circumstances.

Some Fundamentals

Acts 2.41-42

Then those who gladly received his word were baptized; and that day about three thousand souls were added to them. And they continued steadfastly in the apostles' doctrine and fellowship, in the breaking of bread, and in prayers.

This series of lessons begins with the conversion of the follower of Jesus. There is nothing revolutionary there. That lesson contains the very basic, simple fundamentals of getting rid of your sin and turning your life over to Christ. The next lesson concerns local churches, and offers suggestions for including new converts into the life of the congregation (or church plant, or cell group, or class meeting). Again, this is material that seems to many to be intuitive. These are common sense suggestions that seem to go without saying.

This lesson- and the ones that follow- will also fail to add very much new information. Hopefully, this will serve as a reminder. We all need to be reminded of the basic tenets and practices of the Christian Faith.

We turn our attention to discipleship now. It is one thing to become a Christian. We confess Jesus as our Savior, repent of our sins, and he forgives and accepts us. It is quite another thing, however, to become a disciple. Discipleship is a process of growth and change. It includes practices that will lead us closer to God's will for us. There is a serious amount of discipline involved. (Notice the similarity in those words- disciple, discipleship, discipline.)

The outline for these lessons is simple. We will, first of all, spend some time thinking about what we do in the area of discipleship. There are responsibilities that we must assume to grow in faith. These practices, or disciplines, are some of the very things that increase our faith, and accelerate our growth.

Secondly, we will take note of the things that God does in the process of discipleship. Some of these items come in the form of a covenant/ commitment and response. For example, if we are faithful to do God's will in the area of ministry he will add to the church. There are other things, blessings that come from God simply because he is God and he loves his people.

All of these disciplines and blessings are drawn from the Pentecost narrative of Acts 2.41-47. These studies will serve as an exposition of these verses with a focus on the implications for spiritual growth and health. Our spiritual health comes from being close to God, getting to know him and what he wants from us and for our lives. The way we learn these things is from his word. And if our particular interest is in Christian discipleship and growth, the most obvious place to start is with the beginning of the Christian church.

Part Two: Discipleship

Discipleship I: Bible Study

...they continued steadfastly in the apostles' doctrine. **Acts 2.42**

Bible study seems to be the most important thing that a Christian ought to be doing. At least, it appears as the first item in Luke's account of the activities of the very first Christians. The church was born on Pentecost when the Holy Spirit filled and empowered the believers and disciples who had gathered in Jerusalem. Because of this encounter the church was given an identity and a mission. They were (perhaps we should say, she- the church- was) unified in their mission and purpose as the redeemed followers of the Christ. And they were given the responsibility of sharing the message of the Messiah and recruiting new members to the faith.

What is documented here are the details of the earliest days of the church, beginning with "the apostles' doctrine." This, of course, is a reference to what we refer to today as the New Testament.

We have to remember that in the very beginning Christians believed that Jesus would be returning very soon. So soon, in fact, that many of the earliest believers changed their lives to accommodate this expectation. They quit their jobs. They withdrew from society. They were sure that they would be leaving earth before they died.

This had an effect on the apostles and the leaders of the church as well. Since the whole church would be raptured soon, it seemed that there would be no need to write the stories of Jesus, the doctrines of the church or expectations for behavior. If a teacher can tell people about Jesus until Jesus comes back, he doesn't need to record that history.

However, as time went on and Jesus' return was delayed it became imperative that the stories were recorded for the sake of posterity. If these teachings weren't written down they would be lost upon the deaths of the apostles. So the teachings were recorded, circulated, collected and canonized. Today these writings are the basis of what we call the Bible.

So we begin with the assumption that the earliest Christians spent time learning from the apostles. In subsequent generations we learn the teachings of apostles by studying the Bible.

- **Study the Bible by reading it each day.** The amount of verses or chapters you read and the number of minutes that you spend in the Bible are less important than the act of reading itself. Commit yourself to reading the Bible and then start doing it.
- **Develop a plan for reading the Bible.** There are many Bible reading plans and schedules available online and in other places. Find one that will work for you. If all else fails, commit yourself to reading one chapter each day.
- **Attend a Bible study or Sunday school class.** Learning the Bible with other people will enhance your understanding, aid you in comprehension and increase your level of commitment through greater levels of accountability.

Discipleship II: Christian Fellowship

...they continued steadfastly in the apostles' doctrine and fellowship... Acts 2.42

A second component of growth in discipleship is Christian fellowship. And unfortunately, this one is often overlooked, taken for granted or ignored completely. To grow in the Christian Faith we all need to take seriously what it means to be a believer in Christ in the context of a loving community.

The foundation of all Christian life is the individual's relationship to God. This is the primary focus of Christian fellowship. We can never minimize the importance of fellowship with our Creator. He longs to be in fellowship with us and it is out of this relationship that all good things come. We will talk more about this aspect of the discipleship process when we approach the topic of prayer, but for now we should be reminded that the Holy Spirit is given to every believer. We have the opportunity to be in communication with God at any time. Not only that, we should also remember that the purpose for which Jesus came to earth was to "seek and save the lost." (Luke 19.10) He wants to be with us.

With all of that being said, let us turn to the fellowship that occurs- or should occur- in our churches, our study groups and our families. This fellowship is not to replace any evangelistic effort that followers of Jesus may be involved in. We are compelled by the Great Commission (Matthew 28.19, Mark 16.15, Acts 1.8) to develop and build relationships (fellowship) with those outside the body of Christ. We need to find a balance between these two facets of fellowship.

- **Christian fellowship is the natural result of following Christ.** As your attitudes and priorities change, you will find that you have many things in common with other believers in Jesus. You will tend to orient your social activities toward others who share your values.

- **Christian fellowship makes evangelism easier and more effective**. As Christians include non-Christians in fellowship activities with Christian groups the positive attributes of the groups are on display.
- **Christian fellowship helps us maintain our Christian Faith.** We receive encouragement, support and correction from others who are following God. It is always easier for humans to live a difficult lifestyle when they are not doing it by themselves.
- **Christian fellowship holds us accountable**. Christian Faith is a covenant experience. That is, we agree with one another that we will uphold the tenets of our faith, support the ministry and lifestyle of a disciple help others do the same.

Discipleship III: Prayer

*...they continued steadfastly in the apostles' doctrine and fellowship, in the breaking of bread, and in prayers... **Acts 2.42***

Let's begin this lesson with the assumption that everyone knows that Christians should pray. I propose a second assumption that I believe to be true. Most Christians do not pray.

Let me clarify that a little bit. Christians don't pray as much as they should. Many devout believers would never think of eating a meal without offering thanks to God for it. Those same followers of Jesus have a standard prayer that they offer before turning in to bed in the evening. They pray for an hour in church on Sunday morning and periodically read through a list of 'needs' that they feel obligated to remember throughout the day. All of these attempts at prayer do qualify, but the one who is praying is still left with nagging doubts about the effectiveness of their prayers. He has salved his conscience by fulfilling some obligations, but does not have the joy of true fellowship with God.

There are many reasons for this.

- Some people have convinced themselves that **they don't have time for prayer**. They are simply too busy to get bogged down with extended periods of prayer. Pray seems like it is not productive work. We cannot point to anything specific that we have accomplished when our prayer time is over. We get the idea that praying is not an effective practice and that time spent praying is definitely not efficient. Get this idea out of your head. There are more benefits to prayer than you can ever imagine. For example, simply slowing down for a few minutes of quiet meditation will increase your peace of mind and general well-being.

- For some people **prayer seems like an empty ritual.** There are certain prayers that are repeated by rote memory, or lists of obligations are kept and adhered to. The 'prayer list' works this way. We give God our wishes, tell him thank you and we think we are done. The person who prays in this way generally feels nothing and changes even less. We should never approach prayer in this way. Prayer is spending time with God in a living and dynamic relationship. Tell him what you want, but be sure to take time and listen to what he wants for your life as well. Prayer should be a two-way form of communication.
- For others- maybe most Christians- **they have just never been taught how to pray.** It is an overwhelming task. They just do not know how to start. I always suggest that people begin to pray simply, in biblical ways. Whenever you pray, for example, worship God. Tell him how much you love him and how important he is to you. Ask him to teach you how to pray and to show you what he wants for your life. And then take some time to listen to him speak.

Here are a few tips for beginning pray-ers. Try one of these each day, but do not let any of them become overly burdensome.

- Increase your daily prayer time, but not by too much. If you currently pray for five minutes, begin to pray for six.
- Be intentional about your relationship with God. Confess your sins. Ask for God to show you his will for your life. Listen to him speaking and follow his lead.
- Find a partner who will pray with and for you.

- Think about God not as some other worldly being, but as a present friend and confidant.
- Continue to pray through your "list," but ask God what he wants you to be praying for.

Discipleship IV: Unity

Now all who believed were together, and had all things in common. **Acts 2.42**

There is an old joke that asks how many Christians it takes to change a lightbulb. The answer is funny and sad. It takes eight. One to screw in the new bulb and seven to form a committee to find out if the change is necessary, and whether or not it will hurt anyone's feelings. It is funny because this is a truthful commentary on the state of the church. It is sad, also because it is a truthful commentary on the state of the church.

Often Christian people, well-meaning, devoted and faithful followers of Jesus, lose sight of the mission of the church and focus instead on their own personal and petty agendas. This should not be. In fact, we can see clearly that the earliest church functioned at a high level because they operated with a sense of unity in all things. That is not to say that there were never differences of opinion, but rather that the mission was the most important thing for these believers. Personal preferences and agendas were always given less importance than the call of God and the work of the kingdom. This should still be the case today.

There is one more thing to think about before we get too far along in this discussion. Although there are steps that we should take, practices we should participate in to make sure that we have unity in the church, we must also recognize that there is a measure of unity that can only be achieved as we receive grace for God himself. That is, ultimate unity in the body comes- sometimes miraculously- from the Lord.

With that being said, let's consider what it means to have a spirit of unity. What are the things that we need to be doing in our personal lives and in our churches to attain and maintain the unity that God wants for his church.

- **To be unified, we need to spend time together.** The more time we spend with other believers, the more likely it is that we will share values, priorities and beliefs with them. Common time leads to affection, concern and ultimately, love.
- **To be unified, we need to be sharing life with one another.** There is more to this than only offering lip service to the concern of unity. Our tendency is to hold people at arm's length to "keep up appearances", if you will. This will never lead to unity. Share your desires, your needs and your love with each other.
- **To be unified, we need to share our resources with one another.** There will be more about this in a later lesson, but for now be sure that material sharing is crucial to the spirit of unity in the church.
- **To be unified, Christians need to be committed to getting along with one another.** This is often a hard thought for anyone. We think that our way of thinking is correct and we often convince ourselves that God has led us to this conclusion. Therefore, anyone who does not believe with me is necessarily wrong, and outside the will of God. To avoid this I suggest two attitude adjustments.
  - Philippians 2.3-4 gives a perfect explanation of this. We should always think about our relationships with others as Jesus would.

"Let nothing be done through selfish ambition or conceit, but in lowliness of mind let each esteem others better than himself. Let each of you look out not only for his own interests, but also for the interests of others."

o If we focus on the mission of the church first, we will have less time and energy to focus on differences between believers.

Discipleship V: Sharing Resources

Now all who believed were together, and had all things in common, and sold their possessions and goods, and divided them among all, as anyone had need. **Acts 2.44-45**

Being a disciple of Jesus Christ is not only about the spiritual aspects of our lives. It is true that Bible reading and prayer (among other things) are essential for Christian faith and growth, but there are more practical and tangible considerations as well. For example, Christians are called to be concerned with the material and financial concerns of others.

This comes across clearly in our focus passage of Acts 2.41-47. These earliest Christians were involved in all of the standard spiritual practices that lead to growth in the Christian life, but the Scriptures are very specific about one potentially uncomfortable aspect of Christian growth. We are to follow the example of the first Christians and share our wealth with others.

To begin with, let's recognize that these Christians "had all things in common." I am going to address the financial and material aspects of this example, but for now I want you to understand that the first Christians had similar or common values and priorities. In the previous lesson we looked at this in more depth, but it is important to note that they were "in one accord." (Acts 2.1-2) These Christians were together and they were in agreement. There is great value in shared beliefs and priorities.

The second thing that I want you to note is that they sold what they had. It seems that none of the earliest believers were necessarily wealthy. They did not have stores of cash or other assets that could be exchanged easily. They took account of their resources and sold what they could. Note especially that no one was compelled to participate in this procedure. In fact, in Acts 5 we find the story of Ananias and Saphirra. These two, pretending to be full participants in this sharing sold their land, but did not give all the proceeds to the church. They were punished not for keeping some of the funds, but for lying about it. (Acts 5.3-4) It is not mandatory that people participate in this sharing. But those who are filled with God's Spirit and long to be more devoted followers of Jesus will sell and share.

We should also pay attention to how the proceeds from these sales was divided among the believers. No one became wealthy as a result of this. In fact, it seems as though the people were not even made equal. The verse is very clear that assistance was provided to those who had needs as the needs arose. Not everyone should always be treated in an identical way to everyone else, but everyone should always be treated fairly.

Finally, let's note that the church is a community. A community has many things in common. Do you see that this is the same word? For the church to continue, we must share our finances. For disciples to grow, they must share their finances. This is fundamental to the Christian ethic.

Discipleship VI: Ministry

...and sold their possessions and goods, and divided them among all, as anyone had need. **Acts 2.45**

I have often claimed that there are four primary things that all Christians must participate in if they are planning to grow in their faith. Those four things are Bible study, prayer, Christian fellowship and ministry. We have already looked briefly at the first three. No we must be careful to not overlook the fourth. Ministry is often neglected because it is seen by many to be difficult and uncomfortable. But I believe that without question, ministry is the most effective and fastest way to grow in your faith. When you get yourself into a ministry situation you cannot help but grow closer to Christ.

The passage at hand has several significant references to the ministries practiced by the first Christians.

- **These earliest believers in Jesus shared miracles with others.** They prayed for the sick and saw the sick healed. They asked for signs and they were done. Because of their relationship with God they were filled with faith and consequently wonders abounded. I do not have an answer for why God does not always intervene as a result of our prayers. I have prayed for many who were not healed. I have asked for signs that I never received. I don't understand why this is so. But I do believe that God calls me to continue praying for those who are sick, hurting and in need. An important facet of the ministry that I am called to (you are called to it as well) is to pray for signs and wonders.

- **The first Christians shared their money and other resources.** We discussed this in the previous lesson, but it bears repeating here for emphasis. Our finances are an important part of ministry. We can give to those who are in need, or use what we have to support other ministries. In either instance the gospel goes forth and God is glorified.
- **The first church was filled with people who shared Christ.** This includes evangelistic ministry, but it goes well beyond that as well.
    - We share Christ as we participate in and lead worship. There are many individuals who are called to do the work of preaching, testifying, teaching and leading others in the worship of God. Although there are many people who are intimidated by the thought of public speaking, you should consider that it is possible that God has called you to this nonetheless.
    - We share Christ as we participate in a teaching ministry. In this case, teaching is not necessarily in a classroom or congregational setting, although, certainly those instances definitely apply. You are doing ministry as you teach your children, friends, neighbors and family members about the things of God.
    - We share Christ as we participate in every godly conversation. And for a Christian, every conversation should be filled with the grace and holiness of the Lord.
- **These early believers were men and women who shared themselves with others.**

- They offered their time to those who were in need. You should never be too busy for other children of God. And in many cases taking the time to listen to someone else is the greatest form of ministry in which you can participate.
- They offered their concern for others. Time alone is not enough. Christians in ministry are genuinely concerned- emotionally and spiritually- for other people. And keep this in mind: The people around you know when your concern is real and when you are merely "putting on a show."
- They offered their love for others. God teaches us that when he changes our lives that he gives us a heart full of love for others. Do not be afraid to show and share that with everyone you meet.

Discipleship VII: Meeting Daily for Worship and Teaching

*So continuing daily with one accord in the temple, and breaking bread from house to house... **Acts 2.46***

As a pastor I often joke about how so many of my parishioners seem put upon to attend worship regularly. In fact, there are a lot of them who feel like they are doing God a favor by showing up for an hour each week. When my people complain about how long the worship service lasts, I often respond by saying something like, "You told me what time the service started. No one ever told me what time it was supposed to be over."

There is a problem with this though. Not only is it wrong to limit the amount of time we give to God on Sunday, it is also not enough to limit worship to one day each week.

Before we descend into an exaggerated explanation of how busy we are, or a defense of our family time, let's be very clear about something. The most important thing that you can give to God is your heart. If you are completely committed to him you are in good standing before the Father. (I believe that a total commitment to Christ will lead to frequent and extended times of worship, but that's a completely different point.) You do not have to attend worship to be a Christian. But if you are a Christian, you will certainly prioritize your time and the frequency of your worship.

And that leads us to this instructive portion of narrative. The very first Christians worshiped every day in the temple. This would roughly correspond to modern believers attending worship at church every day. This was likely an informal gathering, but a meaningful one nonetheless. It would have to be an experience filled with emotion and value to keep people coming every day for extended periods of time.

But not only were they worshiping together on a daily basis at church, their worship times overflowed into home meetings that included fellowship and even observances of holy communion. I don't believe that this is the same as current expressions of cell groups or Bible studies. Perhaps the house church movement of the last decade is more appropriate. Christians were constantly and consistently worshiping God together wherever they were.

Finally, let's observe the quality of their worship. They were "in one accord." This means quite simply that they shared their values and priorities. Their hearts were set on worshiping God and nothing was going to distract them from that. If you have ever experienced the unity of heart that can only come to a congregation in the midst of the total surrender of worship, then you have known a taste of what caused these believers to long to worship all the time.

Discipleship VIII: Holy Communion

...continuing daily with one accord in the temple, and breaking bread from house to house...

Acts 2.46

It may not be completely obvious that the first Christians were celebrating Holy Communion in this passage. After all, a case could be made that "breaking bread" simply means that the followers of Jesus were taking meals together during their periods of fellowship. That would not necessarily be an injustice to the text at hand, but it would definitely diminish the significance of the ongoing, daily presence of Christ in the church.

We know, for example, that by the time Paul was writing his epistles- sometime in the middle of the first century, perhaps 20-30 years after the events that this passage describes- the sacrament of Holy Communion was well established even in mission outpost churches like the one at Corinth. For a practice to be so firmly grounded in the practice of the church at such an early date, we must assume that Communion was observed from the beginning. So when we read that they were breaking bread from house to house, we can be confident that at least one facet of meaning is that these believers were obeying the command of Jesus to continue eating and drinking in a commemoration/celebration of the Last Supper.

With that in mind, we ought to understand the significance of Holy Communion for the Christian and for the church. There are real, significant and spiritual implications to the heartfelt observance of the Lord's Table.

- **Communion integrates the presence of Christ** into the life of the individual Christian and the entire local body of believers. When we receive the body and blood of Christ, we are inviting the real presence of Jesus into our lives. And when we do this in concert with the whole congregation the significance of this cannot be underestimated. It is imperative that Christ be welcomed in the life of the church and its members, and communion is a way that we can do that symbolically, but also spiritually.
- **Communion inspires fellowship in the community** of believers. To begin with, consider that the word communion comes from the same root words as community, unity, common and united. When we do this together, we are exemplifying the wishes of Jesus, who wanted his church to be one. There is the potential for important spiritual breakthroughs when brothers and sisters in Christ break bread together-even greater potential than private times of prayer and devotion. Together we support one another and build up the entire body of Christ.
- **Communion invites the presence of the Holy** Spirit. Individual Christians were never intended to live the Christian life in isolation. That is why God put us in congregations. Churches were never intended to minister and disciple believers on their own. This is why God sent the Holy Spirit. As we join our hearts at the Lord's Table we unite in God's will. And when we are together, we can be sure of the presence of the Holy Spirit, the Great Comforter, in our lives and in our congregations.

Discipleship IX: Praising God

Praising God and having favor with all the people. **Acts 2.47**

We have spent a little time previously considering the worship of the early Christians. They were not averse to gathering regularly (daily) to offer their worship to God. But I think that in this situation we should think about more than the basic elements of worship.

- At this point we should not concern ourselves so much with the frequency of worship. Although we should never neglect opportunities to worship either corporately or privately, there are other issues to think about.

- It would do us good if we were not consumed to distraction with the place of worship. Although a chapel or a cathedral is a beautiful and dramatic place to worship, it is not the most significant factor in our service to God. For we can worship in our homes, in the marketplace, or in the forest. Do not become so committed to a location that you neglect the worship itself.

- Don't become pre-occupied by those who are your companions in worship. It is wonderful to worship with others, and it is even more so to do it with friends, family members and those with whom you have a long history. Remember that worship does not require anyone other than yourself and your Lord.

- I am of the opinion that the content of our worship- that is, the style, the length and the "performance"- are of less importance to God than they are to us. Do not focus so hard on what you are doing in worship that you miss out on who you are worshiping.

It is imperative that we not only think about the details of worship- the time, place, content and congregation- but also the heart of worship. I believe that we need to consider the quality of our worship.

By quality I do not mean to suggest that we should have only professional singers, or the most articulate preachers. When I speak about the quality of our worship I am referring to the attitude with which we seek to honor God. Are we offering our best to him, or only what we believe that we can spare? Is our desire to praise, worship and honor God with all our efforts, or do we approach him out of a sense of obligation or guilt? Is worship a ritual that we practice out of habit, or a life-enriching exercise that we look forward to and benefit from?

On the bottom line, we can summarize by asserting that worship is a relationship with God that reflects the attitude within the heart of the worshipper. Therefore, give of your best to the master.

Discipleship X: God Gives the Holy Spirit

...you shall receive the gift of the Holy Spirit. Acts 2.38

We have looked at things that we, disciples of Jesus, must constantly be working on. Although grace is free and our salvation cannot be earned, we do have responsibilities in the Christian life. We cannot coast along hoping that we are good enough, or faithful enough. But it is important to realize that this is a relationship that we are involved in. There are expectations put on me as a follower of God, but I can be sure that God will behave in several ways that are to my benefit. We turn now to some of those.

The first of these is that God will fill us with his Holy Spirit. There are many implications to this promise for the believer in Christ. In fact, there is so much involved in the work of the Holy Spirit that we cannot pretend to cover it all here. Other authors and teachers can be sought out to learn more about many aspects of the ministry of the Holy Spirit in the life of the believer. Here we will pay only cursory attention to the following.

- **The Holy Spirit offers the believer gifts**. There are several 'spiritual gifts' mentioned in the New Testament (Romans 12.6-8; 1 Corinthians 12.7-11; Ephesians 4.11, and 1 Peter 4.10-11). Each of these passages lists gifts of the Spirit, but they are all different from one another. That seems to suggest that none of these is an exhaustive accounting. In fact, we could easily (and justifiably) assume that there may be some gifts that God offers through the work of the Holy Spirit that are mentioned nowhere in the Scriptures. This is not to suggest that we should go searching for some new and dramatic experience with the Lord, but rather that we need to be open to the fullness of God's work all the time. One note of caution: true gifts of the Holy Spirit will always point individuals to Jesus. The Holy Spirit does not exalt churches, individuals, or even the Holy Spirit himself.

- **There are fruits of the Spirit evident in the lives of true believers in Christ** (Galatians 5.22-23). There is some controversy over whether there are nine fruits of the Spirit, or one fruit of the Spirit with nine attributes. That debate is beyond the scope of this brief summary. Suffice it to say that the believer in Jesus, the one filled with the Holy Spirit will also be filled with love, joy, peace, etc.
- **There are also other works and manifestations of the Holy Spirit** in the life of the believer. For example, the Holy Spirit operates as a Comforter for those who are grieving. He is a counselor for those who need direction. He gives boldness to those who need to speak up or be strong. He is a guide for those who have lost their way. And he is a companion for those who are lonely.

The last note that I will offer concerning the Holy Spirit and his work in our lives is that he is always working toward building the Kingdom of God. He is constantly concerned with building up the body of Christ. And he consistently exalts Jesus.

Discipleship XI: God Forgives our Sin

*Repent... for the remission of sin. **Acts 2.38***

We have already discussed the forgiveness of sins and the faith of the believer in an earlier section. But there is more to say about being forgiven. There is no question that this is a sovereign and gracious action of God alone. He offers us forgiveness and grace through no human merit whatsoever. One of the benefits that the Lord affords to those that follow him is complete cleansing from sin and healing our guilt. In fact, he not only forgives and heals, he forgets that our sins once they have been forgiven. And although this is completely true, we still need to realize that there are steps we must take to appropriate this miraculous work of grace.

Do not forget that the single most important factor in obtaining forgiveness is repentance. I will not belabor this point, but remember that repentance is more than simply being sorry. Being sorry for your sins is only the starting point of forgiveness. To activate the work of God's grace in your life, you must apologize for your misdeeds. You must recognize your sins and ask God for his forgiveness, but there is also an implied resolution to not commit those sins ever again. When we repent we are promising God that we are making changes in our lives. I will sin no more.

Once that is accomplished, we get to a place that is a little more complicated. I have found that Christians, at least in the west, are pretty good at repenting. However, we have some difficulty receiving forgiveness. I believe that a lot of this has to do with pride and our mistaken notions of self-reliance. There are four simple steps that anyone can take to overcome this problem.

- **Receive forgiveness.** For many people it is hard to believe that we can be forgiven. After all, I know the depth of my sin and the extent of my violations of God's law. I know that there are a lot of people who are holier than me, more deserving of God's grace than me. But there comes a point when I must simply receive the forgiveness that God offers by faith. I may not understand it, but I receive the acceptance and forgiveness of God.
- **Forgive yourself.** The idea of forgiving myself is closely related to receiving forgiveness. But whereas receiving forgiveness is an act of faith, forgiving myself is an act of my personal will. There is guilt associated with all manner of sin. A good deal of my guilty feelings of conscience comes from the Holy Spirit. But when God forgives me, that guilt, the part that comes from God to inspire me to holiness, is taken away. However, my own feelings of condemnation, defeat and despair remain unless I am able to overcome them. I have known people who have lived for years with feelings of guilt that they impose on themselves. Don't do that. God has forgiven you. You should forgive yourself.
- **Release your guilt and your guilty conscience.** Many people hold onto a grudge like it was an award. They will not allow that someone else can or should be forgiven. Others hold onto bitterness and jealousy until it consumes their souls. I want to make sure that you do not hold onto the guilt that you have. God has forgiven you. You have forgiven yourself. Now release all that pent up guilt.
- **Have faith in the grace of God.** Finally, believe that God's grace is sufficient to forgive your sins. He has

promised that all our sins will be forgiven. We should take him at his word. In fact, remember that when we don't receive God's grace and forgive ourselves, we are actually committing yet another sin. The sin of unbelief can easily become our spiritual undoing. Be faithful and have faith.

Discipleship XII: God Fills us with Awe

*Then fear came upon every soul... **Acts 2.43***

I have a great relationship with my father. (With both of my parents actually, but this lesson is about God the Father so we will stick with that metaphor.) My father loves me unconditionally. He is a great cheerleader for me. He supports me in all that I do. He helps me whenever I need it and he is able to, and encourages me when he cannot help. For the first several years of my life he supported me emotionally, physically and financially. He set me on the right path spiritually, and still counsels me in nearly every aspect of my life. Whenever I have a problem, he is the first person I call.

This all sounds great, I am sure, but there is one significant problem. I hate to disappoint my dad. It breaks my heart when I have let him down in one way or another. I am not afraid in the sense that I am concerned that he might punish me or otherwise bring some sort of paternal justice on me, but it is hard for me to imagine a worse situation than if he is upset with me. I am afraid of my dad in the sense that he has expectations of me- perfectly reasonable ones, I might add- that I desperately want to fulfill. In modern terms, my fear of my father may be better understood as respect or reverence.

And that is exactly the way we should begin to think about fearing God. It will do us no good to think of God as some supernatural, extraterrestrial overlord bent on keeping us under his thumb. We should view God as the benevolent and loving Father who wants nothing but the best for us, and from us. This attitude of fear- reverence and respect- is made easier because we can be sure that he fills us with awe, the very attitude that I am trying so hard to describe.

Let me offer a couple of tips here.

- **Choose to live in awe of God.** The gift of awe comes from the Lord, but we can choose how to deal with it. The sinful, selfish nature of humanity is to look for explanations and to minimize mystery and the supernatural in every circumstance. Don't let that be the case for you. Revel in the unknown, the miraculous and the awe of all things holy and spiritual.
- **Cultivate awe in your life.** When I was a small child my mother took me for an unannounced visit to my grandmother. Since she did not know we were coming, she chose to view our unexpected arrival as a miraculous gift from God. She was always looking for awe. You and I should be doing the same. Believe that God will be active and involved in your life and look for his work. You will be surprised at the simple and extravagant ways in which God will reveal himself.
- **Pray for a sense of awe in your life.** Although we can rely on God to provide us with awe regardless of our efforts, imagine what he can do with us when we ask for his input. I believe that if it is God's will for us to have awe, we can count on him to give us occurrences and events in our lives to foster that sense of his miraculous nature.

Discipleship XIII: God Gives Signs and Wonders

...many wonders and signs were done through the apostles...
Acts 2.43

We have talked about the work of the Holy Spirit in terms of gifts and fruits. We have considered the awe with which we are to regard God and the ways in which he fills us with that awe. All of that leads us to think about the signs and wonders that God does in us, for us and through us in the church and in the world.

Let me begin this by stating my personal feeling. Signs and wonders, at least in the context of this passage (Acts 2), are qualitatively different than healing, spiritual gifts and other similar mentioned works of the Holy Spirit. I make this distinction because of the many signs and wonders that occur throughout the Bible, but do not fit in any category of spiritual gifts. For example, when God subjected Pharaoh and the Egyptians to the ten plagues that was a miraculous work of God, but was not the result of anyone's spiritual gifting. When Jesus- and then Peter- walked on water he was operating in the realm of signs and wonders, not spiritual gifting.

Now that we have established what signs and wonders are not, let's turn to the characteristics that make events signs and / or wonders.

- **Miracles (signs and wonders) are unexplainable in natural terms.** Biblical miracles are always unexplainable. The same is still true. If there is a logical, natural way to understand a thing that has happened, if it makes sense in the rational way that humans think, then it does not qualify as a miracle.

When God inserts himself and his work into our environment in dramatic ways we know that signs and wonders are happening. Now this is not to say that these miracles will always be of epic proportions. In fact, many people may not even notice the miracle. But the unexplained will always be a hallmark of God's activity.

- **Miracles are never frivolous.** Never allow yourself to pray for miracle solely for the purpose of enhancing your own standing in the church or community. Don't look for signs and wonders that serve to build you up. Miracles are not given for our entertainment or promotion. God works in miraculous ways to fulfill and further his will.

- **Miracles are for the building up of the believer.** There is a spiritual component to signs and wonders that come from God. They are not intended to make the believer greater in terms of status or popular opinion. Miracles will cause people to be more faithful to God, to live more holy lives. Signs and wonders will build up the faith of anyone who is open to the work of God.

- **Miracles are for building up the church and the Kingdom of God.** When miracles, signs, wonders, healing or any other manifestation or gift of the Holy Spirit brings division in the church, know that it is not coming from God. At the very least these things are being used inappropriately. God's work always has a purpose, and it always leads to developing and strengthening the church.

Discipleship XIV: God Gives Gladness of Heart

... they ate their food with gladness and simplicity of heart...
Acts 2.46

Christian people often make one crucial mistake. They sometimes operate under the false notion that God will make us happy all the time. This is a big problem because bad things happen, even to good, Christian people. There will be moments, days, even months or years when happiness will not intersect with your life at all. In fact, it is completely possible that you are a committed follower of Jesus, living for him, being faithful to live according to his will and you are at the same time struggling with depression. I do not want to get distracted into a prolonged discussion about whether or not Christians can be depressed, but I do want to make sure that you know happiness is not guaranteed for the believer at all times.

We can be sure, however, that God has everything under control. In fact, as has been discussed earlier, we are given a sense of joy as we come under the lordship of Christ. Joy is something that the Holy Spirit puts into each believer. Joy allows the Apostle Paul to talk about a feeling of contentment (Philippians 4.11). You see, happiness is external, it is dependent on our circumstances. Joy, on the other hand, comes from within. It is the work of God in our lives. When we speak about "gladness of heart" then, we are talking about what God does in the life of the Christian.

There will be obstacles in your life. You will have bad days. Tragedies and disappointments will come. You will get sad at times, but the joy of the Lord is something that you can hold on to. And even though it will not always feel like God has filled you with joy, you can move forward with faith in the promise that he has. When we are filled with his Spirit, we are given the fruit that includes joy.

There is one more thing to think about before leaving this point. When we are filled with the joy of the Lord, when we have glad and simple hearts, those who do not know Jesus will be attracted to that grace-filled attitude. The joy of the Lord becomes beautiful to those who are outside the fellowship of the church. They see the peace in which we live and are drawn to it. Who would not want to know "joy unspeakable?" (1 Peter 1.8)

Finally, life is better when it is flavored by gladness of heart. Everything is better when the Lord is in charge of our lives. The great days are even greater and the bad days are a little less tragic. The lows are higher when we live for Jesus. Remember that even in the midst of tragedy and trauma we are partnered with the Prince of Peace, the one who gives us joy. Live for Christ and your life will improve in more ways than you can imagine.

Discipleship XV: God Adds Souls

And the Lord added to the church daily those who were being saved. **Acts 2.47**

I have always believed that evangelism was important. In fact, although I do not believe that I have the gift of evangelism, I know that I, and all Christians, have a responsibility to do the work of an evangelist (2 Timothy 4.5). But evangelism is not the extent of our responsibility. We are to make disciples as well.

Let's look at this honestly. We are called to make disciples. It is God who adds souls to the church. Perhaps we have struggled in the church because we have misaligned our priorities. We have focused on evangelism and soul winning, when we should leave those works to God. And since we are focused on evangelism, we lose some of the momentum that we need to build up the body of Christ in the areas of discipleship. We need to be doing the work of an evangelist, but we need to especially focus on creating and growing disciples.

- **Evangelism is a gift.** Clearly, the Bible declares that there are some people who are especially gifted as evangelists. We can see that there are men and women who possess this special ability. I have a great admiration and respect for those who have the skills to share the gospel message and lead another human into a saving experience with Jesus. However, if we are not careful, we can easily become enamored with the gift and those who have it. It is a short step from there to jealousy, envy and outright bitterness.
- **Evangelism is also a task that we are assigned.** Having the gift of evangelism is not the only way we

can experience the joy of sharing new life with others. We are all charged with telling our friends, families, neighbors, co-workers and others about Jesus and his marvelous works. Being gifted is great, but we all have the same job to do.

- **Evangelism is a part of the work of making disciples** (Acts 1.8; Mark 16.15; Matthew 28.19). The church makes disciples. There is a lot to this concept. Making disciples is more than an evangelistic presentation or "pitch." It is more than education, behavior or belief. It is all of those things and more. We make disciples by helping others to live more faithfully and being more like Christ himself. Building up the body of Christ means that we are building up everybody.

- **Jesus makes converts and adds them to the church.** Here is the bottom line of my point on evangelism. God does it. Don't miss this. The Apostles and the other first century Christians were faithful. They did what was expected of them, and probably even more. But on that first day of church history the Bible records that "the Lord added to the church." Evangelism is ultimately a sovereign act of God whereby his grace meets the needs of a single individual. I cannot force anyone to receive God's grace. I certainly cannot place my preferences on the will of God. He does it. Jesus does evangelism.

And here is the rub. When the church is faithful, it will grow. When we are growing in our faith, and when we are encouraging faithful discipleship in others, we will experience the work of God adding to the church. That's who God is. That is simply what he does.

Discipleship XVI: God Grants Favor with Others

...having favor with all the people. Acts 2.47

There are very few things in the life of the human that are more fulfilling and life-giving than being appreciated, respected and loved. By faith we believe that we are loved by God, but still people long for the affirmation and respect that comes from positive relationships with other humans. God made us this way. We are designed to be in relationship with our Creator and also with other created beings. To accomplish this, we necessarily look and work for making others view us in a positive light. And although there are definitely steps that we can take to facilitate this experience, there is little doubt in this passage that God blesses Christians, those who follow him, with favor among their peers.

Let's first of all be clear that there is much more to the blessing of God than merely financial or material assets. Christians who adhere to a "prosperity" gospel and limit their beliefs and practices to that do themselves a great disservice. I completely agree that there may be times when God blesses us financially. We should be especially attentive to the other ways that God takes care of us- like giving us favor with others, for example.

There are several components to having favor.

- **We will have a good reputation**. Live in the way of Christ, follow his decrees and his example and you will find that you are living a life of integrity. And as you continue in faithful and holy living people will notice. God's grace working within you will create positive feelings about who you are and what you stand for. At the conclusion of my life I long for people to say, "he was a man of God." God will grant that kind of reputation for me- and for you.

- **People will think highly of us.** This is closely related to the idea of having a good reputation. But whereas your reputation has to do with a lifelong consistent faithfulness, when people think well of me it is because God put that thought in their minds. We should live in such a way that we encourage such positive thoughts, but know that God will open doors for his children. Be positive. Be joyful. Make a decision to be a friend to others and to be happy.

- **Outsiders will want to join us**. Ultimately, when God is giving us favor with others, there will be an increase in the adherents to our faith. Happy, blessed people attract people who want to be happy and blessed. The old saying is true: it is easier to draw flies with honey than vinegar. You will have favor with people and the church will grow, because God is at work in your life and church.

Part Three: Evangelism
One Step at a Time

One Step at a Time: Reading One
An Experiment

For all of my life- at least as much of it as I can remember- I have been interested in evangelism. I have studied it, read about it, prayed for it, tried it and even become discouraged because of failures and disappointments in evangelism. There have been extended periods of time when I have been consumed by the work of evangelism. There are many reasons that I believe contribute to my love and concern for sharing the gospel message with other people.

- I grew up being taught, and believing, that every person is lost and needs to hear the message of salvation.
- There is within me a God-birthed love for all people. That love is coupled with a burden that God has given me to reach the world for Christ.
- I am essentially a "bleeding heart" who wants to help everyone. The best way to help anyone is to tell them about Jesus.
- There is nothing that is more exciting for me than sharing my story with someone else, and then seeing that other person begin his new life in Christ.

My list could go on, but you get the idea.

Before I go much further, let me do some clarifying. Evangelism is a spiritual gift. (Ephesians 4.11) There are people who have been given the supernatural ability to share the message of Christ in various situations and with much success. These men and women are empowered to help the church grow and multiply. We see the fruits of the gift of evangelism in dramatic testimonies of mass rallies where hundreds, or even thousands come to Christ, or in the stirring story of the conversion of a notorious sinner. God gives the gift of evangelism.

However, you are not off the hook if you do not have the gift of evangelism. All Christians are expected to do the "work of an evangelist" (2 Timothy 4.5) whether we have the gift or not. Jesus instructed the disciples to spread his message without regard to the giftedness of those same disciples (Matthew 28.19).

I do evangelism because I have a passion for it, but I don't necessarily think that I am a gifted evangelist. I share my faith because I love God. I do evangelism because God asks me to. Witnessing, faith-sharing and testifying (pick your own favorite term) are all signs of our obedience to God and his word. We are all without excuse. We must tell others about our faith, the greatness of God and the grace that he offers to all. In fact, Paul reminds us that there are potential consequences for not sharing the gospel (1 Corinthians 9.16).

This background information has been leading me to some new and exciting ideas in the area of evangelism. In all fairness, these ideas are new to me, but they are not at all new to the larger world of evangelism and evangelists. For example, it is clear in these days that best way to reach new people for Christ is to begin new churches, fellowship groups or faith communities. Church planting, as it is often called, is the most effective way to do evangelism in the USA and around the world. In any case, I believe that there is nothing more exciting than doing the work of evangelism.

Therefore, I am planning for us to take an educational trip together. During this trip we are going to learn about the theory and practice of evangelism, especially as it relates to beginning new Christian congregations. We will look at how we can increase our effectiveness, how to reach more people more quickly and how to reach the unreached and the seemingly unreachable.

You will not be surprised about where we will start, but there can be no other starting place than prayer.

One Step at a Time: Reading Two
Prayer Primer

Church leaders, especially those interested in, and committed to the work of evangelism, must maintain an active and passionate prayer life. And although the nuts and bolts of effective prayer are beyond the scope of this article, we should all be encouraged to re-commit ourselves to the fellowship that comes only through prayer.

It is my firm belief that prayer is simply the act of someone 'being' with, or spending time with God. It is easy to get distracted and disillusioned, however. We can convince ourselves that we are being with God and therefore praying, when in reality we are only being quiet. We may have good and positive thoughts, but prayer requires an active participation in fellowship with Christ. You cannot only "be" with him. There must also be substance, an agenda, if you will.

That leads me to the next problem for praying. Too often we get so consumed with our needs and lists of prayer requests and concerns that we simply tell God what we need. (Unfortunately, the things we think we need are usually only things we want. Be careful that you do not confuse those two. Ever.) We think that once we have covered what we want, prayer time is over. But remember, prayer is communication. And communication takes two parties.

- Share your concerns with God. This is more than reciting a list and making demands. These are needs that come from the heart of the believer. You will find that there are things that you naturally will want to pray over: a sick relative or loved one, a decision that you must make, some sort of accident or tragedy. There will also be things that God reveals to us. He will lay burdens on your heart. This happens especially when God learns that you can be trusted with your prayer time.

- Be sure that you pray about what God is leading you to do in the area of evangelism. If you pray for God to send people to you so that you may share your faith, you can be sure that he will do it. God may ask you to pray for and be concerned about individuals or issues that you have never considered. Lift those all up to the Lord. Romans 8.26 teaches us that God prays through us. We should always be willing to be used in our prayer times.

- Here is one of the most important and overlooked aspects of prayer. Listen to God's voice. For me, to hear something takes no effort. I hear traffic, weather, voices in another room. I can hear all those things because my ears are always working. But just because I hear something doesn't mean that I have paid attention to it. I can tune out sounds that do not interest me or that I hear all the time. Listening, however, takes some work. I pay attention to some things. This is how we should respond to God in our prayer. Make a conscious and concerted effort to engage with God and listen to him.

- There is one more step to listening to God in prayer. Follow the way he leads with acts of obedience. If he tells you to fast, then fast. If he asks you to share your testimony with a friend or family member, then do it. Hearing and listening to God is worthless if we do not follow through by doing what he asks.

Since our point here is to begin to do the work of evangelism, let's put that into practice. Let's pray in ways that will open us to God's direction for sharing our faith. Pray for the following things.

- Pray that God will help you develop a heart for witnessing.
- Pray that God will give you wisdom in developing an effective and winsome presentation of your testimony.
- Pray that God will lead you to those who need to hear your story, and are open to your personality and approach.
- Pray that God will either put you in a community that will serve him in evangelism, or that he will transform the priorities of your existing Christian community.
- Pray that God will send those to you to whom you are to witness.
- Pray that God will send you to the places he wants you to go.
- Pray that God will give you boldness to share your faith, and the assurance that God's word through you will be effective.
- Pray that God will bring in a great harvest of souls. (Luke 10.2)
- Pray that God will send out other laborers into his harvest. (Luke 10.2)
- Pray that God will give you a tender and compassionate heart for those who are not in a relationship with Jesus.

There are many more ways that you can pray in terms of evangelism, but this list will get you started. Now get busy. You have some praying to do.

One Step at a Time: Reading Three
Develop Relationships

The very first step to being effective in evangelism is to develop relationships with people who do not know Jesus. The days have gone away in which mass evangelism was the most effective way to tell others about your faith. And although there is little doubt that most people come to faith because a friend or family member shared with them, we spend very little time or energy working on this. We have neglected the thing that is most important in our work as evangelists.

There are several things that you can do to find, build and develop relationships. But before we consider that, let me give you a warning. Not everyone that you meet and become friends with will accept Christ as their Savior. And, if you are looking at every relationship as a potential 'gold star' on your evangelism chart, you will decrease your effectiveness from the start. People are smart and they can easily recognize when you have an agenda. For that reason, develop relationships with others because you care about them. Jesus had compassion on the multitudes not for anything they could do for him, but because he loved them. We need to be sure that our motivation is always to love people first. Be interested in them.

The first step to building relationships is to establish them. Begin today to look for opportunities to meet people and engage them. There are millions of lonely people in the world. They may not realize it, but they are longing for relationships with other humans. That's you! Open your eyes and you will begin to see people all around you to get to know. There are people at work, at school, at the store. There are neighbors and people that you pass on the street every day.

Let me make a disclaimer here. I am an introvert. It is hard for me to initiate conversation, especially with new people. But I can do it. I have learned a few tricks to help me at this point. I ask a lot of questions, sometimes personal question. I am always amazed at how willing people are to share their deepest thoughts and longings. When I am interested in the lives and concerns of other people, they open up. When you ask those revealing questions, be sure to listen to the response you get. It is easy to start focusing on the next question, or how you can transition the conversation toward a gospel presentation. Don't do it. Focus. Have a conversation.

There is one more thing before we leave this point. Be concerned about others. Don't only pretend to care, actually care. Your new friends know when you are being honest and when you are not. There are too many Christians in this world who are filled with hypocrisy. Don't become like them. Never pretend to be compassionate. If this is a problem for you, pray that God will increase your capacity to be compassionate toward others.

I have been persuaded recently that the foundation stone of all relationships is story. By that I mean that we become emotionally connected to one another by the stories we share together, or by the stories that we hear that move us. Take, for example, the following observations into account.

- The popularity of movies and television programs are an indication of this. Truths- and sometimes propaganda- are communicated to us most persuasively through these media by way of stories.

- We learn and understand history in terms of stories. Although there are facts, dates, people and other things to be gleaned from history, the way that we remember it best is through rehearsing the story that shows us how we got where we are.
- Memories are catalogued and recalled in story segments. Often our memories, especially the oldest ones, are not complete. They are smells, sights and fragments of our lives. But everyone of those fragments points to larger stories, and ultimately the story of our lives.
- Our testimonies are stories of God's work in our lives. We remember the work of God and we tell others about the work of God through our stories.
- The Bible itself is essentially the story of God. We study the Bible so that we can know God and his story better and more fully. It is a collection of books by several authors that gives us the story of creation (how we got here), the fall (what went wrong), redemption and ultimate salvation (Jesus in the Gospels).
- Jesus taught primarily in stories. His disciples and others who followed Jesus learned the values of the Kingdom by listening to and learning the parables that Jesus taught. These were stories that gave listeners insight into the values and priorities of God.

All of that should help us to see stories as great vehicles for building relationships and communicating our faith. There will be more about sharing your personal story in a future lesson, but for now observe the stories in the world around you. Tell stories. And live your story.

Finally, be sure to pray for those you are building relationships with. Pray for them silently as you are sharing your stories. Pray that God will lead the conversations and draw your friend into a saving relationship with himself. But also pray for the needs and concerns of the person that you are sharing with.

I have found that when I tell people that I pray, and when I tell them that I will be praying for them, and when I ask for specific things they would like me to pray about, they almost always open up and share with me their needs. They want people to pray for them. And to most people an offer of prayer is a great sign of your concern and compassion. I only have one caution at this point: if you tell someone that you will pray for them, be certain to actually pray for them.

Developing relationships is not a short term procedure. Anything of value, including relationships, requires long term commitment. Plan on maintaining this relationship forever. Your friend may never receive Christ, but he should always be your friend.

One Step at a Time: Reading Four
Telling Your Story

For many years, evangelical Christians have focused their
outreach evangelism efforts on a system that can be termed
"propositional evangelism." This approach is heavy on
apologetics, or proving the faith. This means that we make
statements, or propositions, that attempt to justify, exemplify or
explain what Christians believe. We have tended to think that if
we can convince someone else to become a Christian by our
profound arguments we will be set. The conversions will start
rolling in.

Now before you think I am dismissing this out of hand, let's be
reminded that even though Jesus taught by using stories, and
even though the Bible is filled with stories, there are an awful
lot of propositional truth statements as well. The Sermon on the
Mount, for example, has no stories. It is the record of Jesus
making a series of statements that support the faith. The Bible
has many faith statements and it is important that we have a
grasp on the truths that the Bible teaches about the Christian
faith. But in terms of the way that 21st century humans think,
bold statements of truth come across as judgmental, uncaring
and preachy.

It is because of this attitude that we need to begin to look at
"narrative evangelism." If we are able to express gospel truths
in terms of story, we will not need to deal with all the
perceived baggage that comes with propositions. We can tell
and live stories.

A corollary idea comes as we transition from the practice of
"cold call" evangelism to building relationships. An earlier

generation of Christians found some success in springing their assertions about Christianity on unsuspecting neighbors, or even strangers. Often these individuals would team up and go door to door to tell others about Jesus. Although there was some success with this method, and there are still some who find value here, a much more effective way to share your faith is by building relationships and sharing what you believe with your friends through stories. People are more likely to take the advice and counsel of a friend than a stranger.

Now, let's turn to a few assumptions.
1. As Christians, we know that we are supposed to share our faith.
2. As humans, we are reluctant to do things that make us uncomfortable.
3. Sharing our faith makes us uncomfortable, so many of us just don't do it.
4. Conscientious Christians feel guilty about not sharing their faith.
5. Even when we try to share with others, we feel incompetent and unprepared.

That covers most of it, doesn't it?

This seems pretty straightforward. A+B=C. But it is not that simple because humans are filled with emotions. We have an understanding of what we should do, how we ought to behave, and what we could say. Sharing our faith may come along with embarrassment, humiliation, or even persecution and punishment. If only it were as simple as it seems like it should be.

The Bible offers some help. (Maybe the Scriptures will only increase your anxiety, but here goes.) The personal experience of the Apostle Paul is that he must share his faith. In 1 Corinthians 6.9 he says "woe is me" if he doesn't witness to others. This may be because he struggles with the same guilt that you and I encounter when we fail to do the work of evangelism. It could be that Paul simply enjoys this work so much that not doing it has a depressive effect on him. We can learn from this. We need to be about doing evangelism. Woe is me (and you) if I don't.

One of the excuses that many otherwise well-meaning Christians make for not evangelizing is that they don't want to be made to feel like an outcast. There is a sense in which the Christian faith will not fit into everyday life. No one wants to be ostracized from their peer group, and so you may determine that it is easier to stay silent. Once again Paul has a response to this. Romans 1.16 tells us that Paul is "not ashamed of the gospel of Christ." He offers no remedy for ridicule or embarrassment that may come from sharing, but reminds us that it is "the power of God," and that it offers salvation. There may be difficulties, but the gospel of Christ is worth the struggle.

I am reminded finally of the psalmist who said simply, "Let the redeemed of the Lord say so." (Psalm 107.2) Nowhere is the Bible especially strict on procedure when it comes to gospel-sharing. The bottom line is that we are encouraged (commanded?) to share our faith. When it comes to witnessing to others we need to remember the admonition of the sneaker company and "just do it."

Internally- in the spirit, if you will- we know that we need to be doing evangelism. The Bible teaches us that we should be sharing our faith. As we observe the world around us, and especially family, friends and loved ones close to us, we can see that there is a definite need for evangelism. People need the good news of Christ.

What follows is a pretty practical way to prepare to share your faith.

> Long version. Prepare your testimony- your faith story- in its entirety. Take no shortcuts. Write out every detail that is important to the flow of the story and that is significant to you. It may take a few attempts, but be persistent. To effectively share your story, you must be prepared to tell your story.
> Elevator version. After you have written the whole thing out, begin to edit it. More than likely, when you have an opportunity to share your faith story with someone else you will not get to give them the whole thing. Prepare a version of your story that will take two minutes or less. Fill it with action and highlights. You can use this story to show others your authenticity and hook them so they will be interested in hearing more about Jesus.
> Write it out. There are shortcuts, but the best way to do this is to write out the whole story. Use the outline that follows and begin to fashion your story. It may take several drafts, but it will be worth it in the end.
> Form a group for practice. This is important. The more you share your story, the more comfortable and effective you will be at it. So find some other Christians who will share this experience with you. Start by reading your testimony to one another. Offer friendly and helpful suggestions for editing. Then improve your story and try it again. Eventually you will want to memorize what you have written so that you can share

it more naturally. Share it as often as you can with as many people as you can.

> Tell someone else about the great things that God has done in your life.

As you are writing out your faith story you may find yourself overwhelmed with details, questions and anecdotes that you want to include. Be careful. You don't want to over-share, but you want to make sure you hit all the important details. There are certain things that you always want to include in your faith story. You might want to use the following outline to cover the most important details. Remember, use your own words as you tell your own story.

- What was my life like before I met Jesus? Begin your testimony by discussing how you lived before you were saved by Christ. Was there sin, loneliness, hurt? Often you will find that unsaved people believe they have no need of God. Begin by showing that you definitely did need God.
- How did I come to know Jesus? What were the events that led you to Christ? Was there a crisis? Did you hit rock bottom? Who told you about Jesus? How did God call you to himself? There is mystery in the process of being saved, but try to show how easy it is to meet him.
- What is my life like now? This process is like a before and after snapshot comparison. You start with the before. Now you have to demonstrate the after. Are you more holy now? Making better decisions? Are your relationships healthier? How about your job? Finances? Being a Christian is not a magic cure-all for every problem, but it does make a difference in life. Be sure to include that.

One Step at a Time: Reading Five
My Story

My life before Christ-

There is really no dramatic 'conversion' to my story. I have no dirt to tell about. There are no terrible sins to confess, tragedies to recount or persecutions to overcome. Life has always been pretty simple and blessed for me.

My parents have always loved and cared for me. Even as an adult I sense their interest in my life and activities. But theirs is not an obsessive or controlling interest. In the truest sense of unconditional love, they have loved me.

As far as I know I have always been in church. As a child I attended church with my family every Sunday morning. On Sunday evenings we attended either youth group, Bible study, an evangelistic service or prayer meeting. Wednesday nights were always devoted to our church Bible study. There were times when there were more church services to attend. At some points there were services on Tuesday and Thursday rather than only on Wednesday evening. And of course, there were one or two revival meetings each year. These were a series of preaching services that would be held every evening for a week or more. And then there was camp meeting in the summer. I was in church a lot.

In fact, I was in church so much that it was all I knew. Of course there was school, and Cub Scouts and Little League baseball, but from my earliest memories my most important friendships, my whole social structure has been centered around church fellowship. This is so true, and so obvious, that at one point I was given a child size pulpit as a gift. I would line up my stuffed animals and dolls in rows and preach to them. That was play time for me. I could never get enough church. First it was forced upon me by my parents, but I quickly claimed a love for Christ and his church as my own.

By now you realize that I don't have a traditional born-again, sinner's prayer type story to tell you. I don't remember when I accepted Jesus as my Savior. I have no idea when Christ became Lord of my life. And that is simply because I have no memory of life without him. God has always been there with me and for me. I have always turned to him for help and guidance. He has always been my source of strength and support.

How I came to know Christ-

Since I don't have the single conversion narrative that we have grown so accustomed to in our evangelical culture, my testimony doesn't fit into an ordinary or traditional pattern. I can't tell you about how I hit rock bottom with my drug habit and turned to God, because it never happened. But there have been a series of 'mini-conversions' in my walk with Jesus.

- Baptism. The first thing that I truly remember as far as walking with Christ is concerned, is that one evening after church, during the prayer time following the altar call, I felt God moving in my heart. It was an emotional church service and there was a lot of weeping, praying and shouting. As I was praying, God was calling me to follow him in total commitment. I had not planned to be baptized that evening, but it was the correct response to what God was saying to me. I was baptized that same night by my father, who was then studying to be a pastor. A great joy of my life is knowing that my dad and I share this experience. He not only led me to follow the Lord, he was instrumental in the sealing of my commitment.

- Altar Calls. Throughout my childhood and teen years, church services nearly always ended with altar calls. The pastor would conclude his sermon by inviting anyone needing prayer to come forward and kneel at the rails in the front of the church. He would then pray with us and lead us to finding what we needed from God. The one incident I remember clearly must have happened when I was about 10 years old. There was another child in the church who was about my age. She and I were pretty competitive with one another and we both went forward. Our time at the altar began as an exercise in holier-than-thou, spiritual one-upsmanship. It was obvious that we were each going to try to pray for longer than the other. However, as I began praying, even with a less than sincere heart, God spoke to me. That became one of the sweetest times of fellowship with the Holy Spirit that I have ever known. (By the way, I have no idea who won the prayer contest.)

- Call to Ministry. When God finally called me into ministry it took three visits. I heard him speaking to me each time, but ministry seemed to me to be a good thing. I liked the idea of being a pastor, evangelist or church leader. That made it difficult because I thought that God only called a person to hard things he didn't want to do. He had to call me three times before I realized it was what I was called to do.

  o The first time that God called me was while I was a teenager attending a youth rally sponsored by one of our local churches. They had hired a youth speaker from a neighboring state and he was really good. During the first service of the rally I decided I really liked the speaker. He was funny and cool. He was not at all like my pastor or any other preachers I had heard. On the second night of the rally I decided I would like to do what the speaker was doing. And there was the problem. God was asking me to do it, but I thought it was my idea.

o God called me again late one night in my room, in my parents' house. I often stayed up later than the rest of my family playing my guitar and worshiping. That night something special happened. As I was offering myself to the Lord, he asked me to follow his leading into a life of service and ministry. But again, I made excuses and ignored the significance of that night.

o The final time I heard God calling me, and thankfully, since I answered, the last time, I was a student in college. I was sitting in an upstairs window on campus studying. Actually, there was not much studying, but a lot of daydreaming. I was watching people pass on the street beneath me when God asked me, "Who will tell them about me?" I knew that he had lots of leaders, pastors and evangelists and so I told him so. He then said to me, "No. You need to tell them. If you don't, no one will." That was the day that I knew God was changing my direction.

My life since I met Christ-

Since my experience before I accepted Christ was so
uneventful- boring even- there is not a dramatic change that I
can illustrate for you. I didn't have terrible, sinful habits or
vices that I no longer participate in. There were no addictions
that I miraculously overcame. There were no spectacular
deliverances or wondrous healings in my life. I can't really
point to anything that someone might think is story-worthy.

But there are a few things that I do know. To begin with, I am
not alone. I always have an advocate. The Lord is with me. He
has promised me as much. He will never leave me nor forsake
me. I am not protected from evil, tragedy, disease or
catastrophe. But when they come, Jesus offers me comfort,
hope, encouragement, strength and endurance. I can survive
through any difficulty because of the power of God.

Here's another thing (and this may surprise you). I sin. I am not
perfect. Oh, I don't do any of the big, bad sins. You know, the
ones that will get you in the newspaper. But I sin just the same.
I harbor jealousy and his brother envy. I covet, I gossip and on
occasion I even lie. I try to get my own way as often as I can,
sometimes even hurting others in the process. But when I fail,
when I sin and come way short of what God wants from me, I
know that is not the end of the story. Sin does not win because
of grace. You see, my relationship with Christ kicks in when I
sin.

First, the Holy Spirit convicts me of my sin and I experience
the guilt and regret that reminds me that I can be- that I am-
better than that. Secondly, God has made a way for me (and
you as well) to be forgiven of our sins. 1 John 1.9 gives us the

powerful assurance that all we need to live in the grace of God, to overcome our weaknesses and our sins with the help of Jesus himself is the willingness to own our sins, confess them to God and ask for his forgiveness.

That's all there is to it. No matter what your sins are, God is able, willing and waiting to forgive you and to fill you with his love and grace. Just like he has for me.

One Step at a Time: Reading Six
Finding Someone to Share With

The hardest thing about doing evangelism is doing evangelism.
Look, we all know that we should do it. We want to do it. We
need to do it. But how do we start? Where do we begin?

There are some problems that make sharing your faith difficult,
or at the very least intimidating. For example, when we share
our faith we become vulnerable and exposed. It is a risk to tell
others about your faith. We get the idea that we Christians are
somehow a minority in the world. (This is true.) And from that
we determine that everyone else is opposed to us and our belief
system. (This is also sometimes true.) By sharing our faith we
are actually advertising the fact that we are a part of this
minority. We let it be known that we are different, not normal.
This opens us to potential ridicule and persecution. All of this
is true, but we should be careful to note, that in most of the
world our fears are greater than reality. We get concerned
about what might happen if our faith is known, and the worst
almost never happens.

Another concern that shapes our willingness (or unwillingness)
to tell others about Jesus is that there is a great chance for
failure. In fact, it has been said that if you share your faith ten
times, one person will accept Christ. This means that you will
fail much more than you succeed. However, we are called to
faithfulness. We must share our faith. There will be failure. We
must keep evangelizing anyway. I have found it to be helpful to
think in long-range terms. A single person may need to be
exposed to the gospel several times before accepting the faith. I
will continue planting seeds and watering them with the faith

that sometime down the line, this person will receive the faith. (1 Corinthians 3.5-9)

Let's also consider what makes for effective evangelistic strategies. There are a million methods that have been tried and proven. I will not disparage any of them. However, we would be wise to think about how to use our efforts most efficiently. The old ways work. There is no question about this. But we need to come to grips with the fact that new ways will increase effectiveness exponentially. That means that we should start new fellowship groups, new worship services, new churches, new outreaches, all in an effort to reach the lost for Christ. It will be easier for new people to join a new congregation than to join an existing one. In a current church, relationships, patterns and habits have all been established. There are customs and traditions that new people will be uncomfortable with. This may lead to difficulties in retaining new people. But if you give those same new believers a new congregation, they can join groups, build relationships and grow in their faith.

When thinking about who to evangelize, think about the following steps.

- Start with the people you know and care about. God has put you in a community. You already know people who do not know Christ. Think about the people in your family. Maybe you should witness to someone you work with, or who attends your school. It could be that God would lead you to someone in your neighborhood. Begin by thinking about who you already have a relationship with.
- Pray about who God will send your way. It is completely possibly, and even likely, that you do not even know the person that you are to share with. Ask God to send someone your way that you can develop a

relationship with. Pray for openings to share the gospel. I have found that when I pray for opportunities to do evangelism, God always answers.

- Meet new people and think about sharing with them. It may require you to do some new things to share your faith. Join a gym. Go to the same store every day and engage the employees in conversation. Become a part of a service organization, club or cultural institution. Meet some people who share your interests. Work on relationships with them and pray about how and when you can share your faith.

One Step at a Time: Reading Seven
The Person of Peace

A key factor in my time in ministry has been a few special relationships that I have had in each location I have served. These relationships have been the greatest blessing in my ministry life. There are people, men and women, who respond in a special way to the message that the Lord has given me to share. I have experienced this in local churches, para-church ministry settings and cross-cultural mission outreaches. There are many possible explanations for why this has occurred, and I have tried to understand them all. However, the bottom line for me is what Jesus referred to as the "person of peace."

In every ministry setting the leader offers the word of God to whoever will listen. In a crowd of 100 people, every individual hears the same message. Just like the seeds that Jesus taught about, different congregation members receive the word in different way (Matthew 13). Some will be like the soil beside the path. The seed cannot take root there. Some people will receive the seed like the soil filled with weeds. The new plants get choked out by the false teachings and idle thoughts that are allowed to grow there. But some people are like the good soil, where the seed can take root, grow and flourish. Those people, the good soil, are the ones who respond to the seed of God's word by hungering for more. They obey God's rules and long for the discipline of ministry and growth in grace. Another way of talking about these parishioners is to say that they are "persons of peace."

Your evangelistic efforts will be most effective and fruitful when you are able to target your energy to the person or persons whom God is preparing. God is constantly at work speaking to the hearts of men and women all around the world. He is truly no respecter of persons (Acts 10.34). There are three relatively simple steps to help you identify the person of peace in your church, your family, your community, or the place that God is sending you.

1. **The person of peace welcomes you and your message**. (Matthew 10.14) Because God is already at work, there are people who want to hear what God has given you to say. Spread your seeds and then look for the soil where the seeds are taking root. The person of peace is open to you. He will be welcoming, supportive and caring. There will be a joy in your relationship with your person of peace.

2. **The person of peace listens to what you have to say.** (Luke 10.16) There are many people who are disinterested in the message of the gospel. Some will pay attention for awhile, but then turn their attention to something else. The person of peace comes to the message of the cross with openness and an attitude of servanthood and discipleship. There is a definite distinction here. If you have ever preached to or taught someone who is motivated to hear and learn from you, and you compare that attitude with a listener who is participating out of sense of obligation you know this well. The person of peace is a joy to teach and disciple while others can easily become a burden.

3. **The person of peace serves and supports you.** (Matthew 10.10) There are some individuals who will receive what you have to say. They will gladly adopt the precepts of the gospel and assimilate the principles

into their lives. These people will become faithful followers of Christ and committed disciples. However, there is a subset within this group of Christians. They will accept you with open hearts and positive attitudes. They will not only receive your word, but they will help you share it with others. They will become focused on caring for your needs, not for the sake of making you greater, but to glorify God build his kingdom on earth.

The gospel needs to be shared. Christians must work at taking the message into the world. There is not a choice in this. In fact, we are to be telling others about Jesus wherever we are all the time. However, it makes sense to find people who will support our work- emotionally and with resources. These people will become partners in our evangelistic efforts. And not only that, these persons of peace will become the next generation of evangelists. For the work of Christ to go on we must find these "persons of peace."

One Step at a Time: Reading Eight
Lots of Seeds

There is a great parable of Jesus in Matthew 13 (Matthew 13.3-8, 18-23). In this story Jesus talks about a sower, a farmer if you will, who begins to plant seeds. You know how the story goes. The farmer begins to plant his seeds in different soils to varying degrees of success. He plants some seeds on the road where it gets trampled. Some gets sown in gravelly, hard ground and dies. Other seeds end up in patches of weeds and thorns where it gets choked out. And still other seed gets left in rich, fertile soil and grows as it should- as the farmer would have hoped.

You know the story well. But I want you to think about it a little bit differently this time around. Do not focus on the soil. If you do, you will tend to try to discern the places where your message has the most potential for fruitful growth. I want you, for now anyway, to think about the seeds that are sown in the story. Notice first of all, that there were a lot of seeds. There were so many seeds that farmer seems extremely generous in his planting. The phrase that Jesus uses is that "some seed fell." That is the kind of terminology that we use when we are less than particular with seed. Some of it fell here, and some of it landed over there. The obvious implication is that the farmer was using a lot of seeds. He was sowing many seeds in a large area over many soils.

Let's pause here and recognize that there is always a place in the church, and especially in evangelism, for using wisdom when deciding how to appropriate our resources. We must be careful that we spend our time and money in places where we will have a greater return on our investment. But this does not diminish the importance of casting the seed in a very broad way. In fact, casting seed is probably a better image than merely sowing anyway. After all, how do the fields get white with an abundant harvest (John 10.35) unless there was an abundant planting of seeds?

The challenge for us then, is to plant lots of seeds. We should be casting them everywhere, all the time. We should do this in terms of:

- Gospel stories. Tell stories about the Bible. Teach others the words that you have learned from God's word. Do not be afraid to apply biblical truth to everyday life. Of course, it will help you do this if you have a firm grasp of the Bible and its contents. You must know what the Bible contains and to get that knowledge you must spend time becoming familiar with it. Read God's word. Listen to others read it. Meditate on it. Sing songs based upon passages of Scripture. Study what wise teachers have had to say about the Bible. And when you have mastered the Bible, talk about it.
- Testimonies. You have already worked on developing your testimony. You have thought about it, written it and shared it with others. Now is the time to truly begin spreading the seeds contained in your testimony. Look for opportunities to share it with your friends. Tell it to people you meet at the store, or at work, or at school, or in a restaurant, or in any other place you might be. Give your story to anyone and everyone who will listen to it.

Finally, get over your inhibitions.

- You might be reluctant to share your faith with people you don't know, because you don't know them. Get over that. Here is your chance to get to know them. Start a relationship and tell them about Christ.
- You might not want to share with people you know very well because you don't want to "turn them off" to your message. I don't want to be too harsh but would you rather they end up living in eternity without Christ? Get busy and do everything you can to keep them from going to hell when they die.

Now get out there. Tell some stories. Plant some seeds. No, scatter seeds everywhere.

One Step at a Time: Reading Nine
The Truth, The Whole Truth and...

In previous lessons I have shared my conviction (or is it a prejudice?) that propositional evangelism is less effective than other forms of faith sharing. I am not ready to change that position, but it is important for all followers of Jesus to have a grasp of the simple truths that relate to the salvation of humans. These truths, or propositions, are essential to helping those who do not yet know Jesus to move to a place of accepting him as Savior.

There are many excellent summaries of the gospel in terms of simple statements of faith. My personal favorite is John 3.16.

- God loves the world. This includes everyone.
- God gives gifts to the world. He has given his son for our salvation.
- We need to believe in him. The way we access his gift is to offer him our faith.
- When we believe, we will live. Our ultimate gift is eternal life.

I remember this simple outline with a poem:

God loves.

God gives.

We believe so

We can live.

There are other tools that we can use as well. The internet is an excellent resource for materials to use as handouts or learning aids. But here we are going to focus on two approaches to propositional evangelism: The Romans Road and The Four Spiritual Laws.

The Romans Road

The Romans Road is named for the book of the Bible from which these verses come. Memorize the verses so that you will be comfortable with using them and sharing them with others.

- Every person is born a sinner. Everyone has sinned and does sin. (Romans 3.10; 3.23)
- The consequences of sin are separation from God and ultimately death. (Romans 6.23) It is impossible for God to have fellowship with sin. If we want to be with him we need to come up with a solution to this situation.
- God made a way out of sin for us. (Romans 5.8) He did not wait for us to get our lives together. God loved us while we were still sinning. The sacrifice of Jesus is just what we need to get out of our sins.
- There is a procedure for getting saved. (Romans 10.9-10) To access the grace of God, to receive the sacrifice that Jesus made for us we must do two things. First of all, we must believe that Jesus came, lived, died and lives again for us. And then we must be willing to make a public confession of that truth.
- Everyone can get saved. (Romans 10.13) There are no special qualifications. No one is too sinful, or dirty, or addicted to get saved. God loves everyone!

The Four Spiritual Laws

Developed by Bill Bright of Campus Crusade for Christ (now known as Cru), the Four Spiritual Laws was designed to focus on the love and grace of God without diminishing the sinful nature of humanity. To do that, Bright began with God's love rather than the state of the sinner. There are many similarities between these two. You will be able to see that right away, but you should also notice the differences.

- Law Number One: God loves you (John 3.16) and has a wonderful plan for your life (John 10.10). The grace and mercy of God is the starting point for this propositional approach to the gospel.
- Law Number Two: Man (humanity) is sinful and separated from God (Romans 3.10, 23). We people have a problem- a big problem- with sin.
- Law Number Three: Christ is God's provision for our sin and separation (John 14.6). There is only one way to be reconciled to God and that is through a relationship with Jesus.
- Law Number Four: Each person must individually receive Christ (John 1.12; Ephesians 2.8-9). Every person is accountable for him/herself and their place in eternity. God has made a way, but we must choose to walk in it.

These three approaches are different in tone and in the Scriptures used. Each one can be effective when used in the spirit and context of the relationships that we have been working on. Study and then practice with each one. After a period of time you will find that you are more comfortable with one of them. When you have memorized your preferred approach you will make great strides toward becoming a more effective evangelist.

One Step at a Time: Reading Ten
Organizing for Evangelism

All of the good intentions in the world may not help you in evangelism. In fact, you can prepare, train, practice and pray, but until you get started and actually share your faith, it will all be for nothing. Oh sure, you will be a better disciple, a more informed follower of God, but no one will be won to God's Kingdom. Until we do the work of an evangelist, the work won't get done.

That is why organization is so important. I am a United Methodist. Methodism was founded by John Wesley (and others) 300 years ago by organizing their beliefs and practices. The very name Methodist implies a methodical organization of everything spiritual. Whether you are a Methodist or not you should begin to organize your life, particularly the areas that have to do with spiritual growth and outreach ministry. The famous leadership adage seems like a trite cliché, but it is also true: "If you fail to plan, you plan to fail."

To begin your process of organizing, you need to put some plans into place. Throughout this study we have talked about finding, developing and growing relationships. Thinking about doing this, wanting to do it, and actually doing it are very different. Every follower of Christ needs to decide when he is going to begin doing evangelism. Pick a date and stick to it. If you choose the first of next month, don't back out. On the first get to work.

You have been preparing, now begin to plan. Think about the practical steps you will take to build relationships with unchurched people. Choose the event or the place where you will develop these contacts. And then get to work.

Another important aspect of your organizing has to be developing a strategy. Formulate a system that you can be comfortable with. Pray about how much time you build relationships before you move conversations toward matters of faith. You will need to continue working on the testimony that you wrote earlier. It will soon become clear that for some situations you will want to emphasize certain aspects of your faith story. For example, if you are in a parents group you might want to talk about how your children were important in leading you to faith. It might be easier for you to develop different versions of your testimony. Remember that the Apostle Paul talked about becoming all things to all men (1 Corinthians 9.19-23).

Remember also that your testimony is not a sacred document. It is meaningful to you, but it is designed to be used. Use it to reach other people for Christ. To that end you might find that you need to include aspects of "propositional" evangelism to it. For example, when you are discussing your life before Christ, you might want to mention that everyone is sinner and needs God (Romans 3.23).

Finally, since starting something new tends to be the most effective means of doing evangelism, organize your new thing. Think about a fellowship group that can meet at your local coffee shop. You might plan and organize a Bible study or prayer group. Maybe you will invite some friends (Christians and non-Christians) to a barbeque.

Low pressure. High value. New content. These are the things that will lead to success in your faith- sharing adventure.

One Step at a Time: Reading Eleven
Keep on Growing

There are several important factors to maintaining your effectiveness in evangelism. It be foolish to say one is more important than another, or that this practice is more essential than that one. But there can be no doubt that you will never be effective if you do not make an intentional and concerted effort to grow- spiritually and intellectually- and continue growing.

It was my uncle who taught me that if you are not growing you are shrinking. That is, if you are not moving forward you will necessarily be moving backwards. A good illustration is the escalator. You know the escalator, right? It is the electric, moving staircase. You step onto the escalator on one floor and it gently transports you to the next. It moves all the time. Have you ever played on an escalator, though? For fun try going down an escalator that is moving up. Here's the thing: you have to keep moving or you will end up where you started.

Your whole spiritual life is just like that. You can't take a break. You have to keep moving and growing. If you don't, you will die.

So let me offer some suggestions about how you can keep growing in your knowledge of God and his ways.

- **Keep reading.** You should read everything. You should read all the time. Especially read the Bible, but you also need to read other things as well. If you want to share your faith with unsaved people you have to read what they are reading. Make sure to stay up to date on current events in the world and particularly in your neighborhood. Read the local newspaper. Learn what is going on around you. Try to figure out the beliefs and priorities of those you hope to reach.

- **Learn the culture and history of your community.**
There are many ways to do this. Start with any local history books, travel guides or historical societies or museums. Get to know people who are involved in cultural and historical aspects of the area. The local library is a great resource to learn about people and places around you. Every community has its own language and values. Pay attention to these. You may not agree with them, and you don't have to subscribe to them, but you must know what they are.

- **Listen to the teaching and preaching of other respected Christian leaders.** Find out what God is doing in the ministry of others and learn from it. Enjoy and be blessed by the anointing that is on someone else. This sort of "apprenticeship" cannot but help you to be become more faithful and successful in your evangelistic efforts.

One Step at a Time: Reading Twelve
No Lone Rangers

There is an old image we have here in America. There is a single horseman who travels the country side righting wrongs, advocating for the powerless and offending those in control of the structures and finances of the world. There is a mythology that has grown up around the Lone Ranger, but we Americans love him. We like the Robin Hood attitude of taking up for the underdog. We appreciate the fact that he speaks out for those who have no voice. But most of all, he has become a hero for us because he does it on his own. After all, he is the 'Lone' Ranger.

The Bible- and Christian theology- teaches us that every person is selfish. That is, we all struggle with sin in our lives. Basically it means that we want to solve our own problems and clean up our own messes. There are two significant issues here that we need to get over. First of all, we make messes and create problems. That is what people do. We sin. We all sin. Don't think you are special. You sin too. Secondly, we want to be the good guy who rides in to save the day. We want to be the wonder-working superhero who makes bad things good. We want to right the wrongs and punish evil doers. And if we can do it all by ourselves all the better.

But for as much as we want to be able to do all this on our own, we have not been made to work that way. God has built us to be in relationship and community with other people. You work better when you are on a team. Others are more effective when you are helping them. This is not just a good idea, it is a God idea.

That means that networking is a key. Everyone you know is a contact. God has put people into your life purposely. There are no accidental or coincidental acquaintances. God has something great in mind for you. Start by changing the way you categorize people. There are only two types of people in your life.

- There are people that will make you better. Some of your friends and acquaintances will challenge you to work harder, pray smarter, be more holy and serve God more faithfully. They will be an example for how you should live, or they will inspire you to be better so that you can be an example for them.
- There are people that you can help to be better. You need to think about how you can be an encouragement to others. Become a mentor, a Christian mentor to someone new and growing in the faith.

Now you should be ready to think about who God has given you. Who do you know who needs to know Jesus? Who do you know that can help you to be a better disciple? Start to evaluate your relationships so that you can be a more effective evangelist.

Just so you don't get disillusioned with all this networking talk- remember that we are leveraging our relationships not for our personal financial gain or for some sort of business or social success. We are working on our relationships for the glory of God and the advancement of his kingdom.

Now think about how you can serve someone else and their ministry. If it is true that all believers are in this together, and if it is true that our priority is the work of God, we should all be able to work together. Put yourself in a position to serve the vision God has given to them. It will be exceedingly exciting and satisfying when we can support one another without regard for who gets credit for the victory. After all, it is all for Jesus.

Part Four: The Church Planting Vision

The Church Planting Vision: A Call to Action

The church is in a rut because we believe that the world should come to us. We sit back and wait for the lost and hurting to come to our worship services and our programs. Then we get frustrated because we are offering all these great opportunities and no one is coming. There are too many options (distractions) for most people to even realize that they need Jesus, let alone church. That is why it is time to make some changes.

The church must do things differently to reach the world.

- **First of all, the church must go to where people are.** After all, this was a command of Jesus (Matthew 28.19). If people do not come to us, it does not remove our responsibility. We must reach people, wherever they are.
- **We need to get over our traditions and rituals.** For the last 30 years there have been arguments about appropriate music in church and worship settings. That dispute is nothing compared to what we need to be discussing. Where can we have worship? What makes spiritual growth? Do we need to sing? Do we need a sermon? How can we be more accountable?
- **Our concerns with proper authority, responsibility and offices are probably hindering more than helping us when reaching new people.** We need to consider calling, gifts and passion when assigning and accepting leadership rather than education, experience and political affiliation.

At least for my lifetime there will be a church, at least in the traditional understanding of church. However, the church will continue to decrease in attendance, in importance and relevance. The Kingdom of God will not decline, however. The Kingdom of God will march on. The question for us is will we be marching along.

Church Planting: Not a New Idea

Small groups are definitely not a new idea. Jesus led a group of 12. The first Christians met in small groups in homes (Acts 2). John Wesley saw the value of groups nearly 300 years ago. They all understood that people need community. The same is true today.

It seems clear that true and deep life change will happen best in the context of a small group of like-minded Christians who will encourage one another, as well as emphasize accountability to each other. Not only that, I believe that the best avenue for reaching the pre-Christians in our communities is through just such a small group. This means that the group must balance some things.

- **The group must be non-threatening**, even as it is rigorous in its expectations and accountability. Accountability can never be used as a weapon or a tool for judgment. It must be used to encourage and love all members.
- **The group must be focused on the spiritual growth** and development of each member, even as it seeks to include new members.
- **The group must be social in nature**, even as it tries to ensure that all meetings are filled with content.
- **The group must be informal**, even as it makes sure that it includes the basic elements of its existence.
- **The group must have a leader**, even as it seeks the equality of all members.
- **The group must have a design and a direction**, even as it allows its members to discern where God is leading them.

- **The group must be a part of the church**, even as it becomes its own 'mini-church'.

This is not a new idea. But perhaps moving the small group outside the church will bring about new results.

Church Planting: A New Beginning

As we begin this new endeavor of reaching people through groups outside of the church, we should focus on making some commitments. When you make your plans, consider the following "resolutions".

- I am going to pray that God will lead me and help me to do all that is right.
- I am going to pray that God will lead me to the right time and place to host a mini-church/ small group.
- I am going to pray that we will start at the right time.
- I am going to pray that the right people will be included in the mini-church/ small group.
- I am going to pray for the right program, curriculum, etc.
- I am going to pray for the right people to help lead this mini-church/ small group.
- I am going to pray we will have the right priorities.
- I am going to pray for all aspects of recruiting and planning.
- I am going to pray that God will bless this work.
- And most of all, I am going to pray that I will do what God wants.

Church Planting: A New Way

So what is the church? What does it do? Is it broken? How should we fix it?

I am not sure that I can answer any of those questions, but I can take a stab at figuring out my own life and ministry.

I believe that the church is a community that exists to meet needs and to know God. At least, that's what it should be. Too often, as we are all aware, it meets no one's needs and would not know God if He showed up for the 11am service. Thankfully, he doesn't show up at those services very often.

Instead our churches are filled with the status quo. We do ministry not for the sake of pleasing God or meeting the needs of people, but for the comfort of those who attend its performances/ services. We worship like our ancestors did 100, 200, 400 years ago, and are surprised when people nurtured on technology, communication, innovation and speed are not thrilled with what we have to offer. We should be ashamed.

The problem is that I am not sure that anything can be done for the established church. It would be better said that the established church does not want anything done for or to it. Those Christians are happy with their lives and amazingly unconcerned with the lives of others. What a tragedy. That is why it is time to circumvent the established church.

What I am about to propose is not new. It is not an indictment of existing structures, fellowship groups or denominations. I believe that the 'New Way' can be used in every congregation where even one Christian seeks renewal and the blessing of Christ.

I propose that every Christian work toward planting at least one mini-church/ small group. This mini-church can serve within the existing structure of the church to be a renewing agent. Each mini-church should include both Christians and not-yet Christians. It could meet in a home, a restaurant, a coffee shop, a workplace, a dorm room or a shopping mall. The mini-church should meet at least bi-monthly. For the sake of consistency, a regular meeting time and place on a weekly basis would be best. Each meeting of the mini-church should include the following:

- **Friendship**- Mini-churches should be a place where all people can share their problems, their triumphs and their struggles. There should be mutual support and concern. Although sin should be examined and condemned, persons need to feel welcomed and loved. In addition to sharing, there should be a measure of accountability. For growth in Christ to occur, we must submit to the challenge of others. There must be an allowance for sharing, visiting, catching up in interpersonal relationships. Fellowship is what bonds the members of the faith team together. It would be good to include a meal or other refreshments. The faith team that meets at a coffee shop or restaurant is in a perfect position to fulfill this need. There should be a sense of openness during this time. Everyone should feel welcomed and free to share. The faith team is no place for judging or criticizing. Support, concern and love are all appropriate.
- **Nurture**- Each mini-church should seek to build up each participant in the mini-church. That should be

done through regular times of prayer, worship and teaching. Although these times will be less formal than in the traditional church setting, they are more important than ever. Roughly one third of the time in the faith team should be devoted to spiritual growth. This could include singing, Bible study, prayer, sharing of sacraments, Bible reading, meditation and more. Accountability is a big thing here. There should be an assigned Scripture reading for the meeting. Everyone should share their insights and impressions on the selected text. Although the faith team is in essence a mini-church, pains should be taken to avoid a traditional church-style worship experience. Another good resource for the discipleship segment could be video teaching. There are many excellent and thought-provoking, discussion stirring videos available.

- **Outreach**- Mini-churches need to be groups that purposefully reach out to others. This will be accomplished in many ways. One of the most obvious is that not-yet Christians are involved in every aspect of the mini-church life. The existence of the mini-church is itself an outreach. Additionally, each mini-church should be intentional about doing ministry to others in need. This might include mission trips, community service or evangelistic programming. In the faith team setting ministry will primarily be devoted to prayer. Team members should pray for one another and specific needs of the group. There should be an expectancy that God will meet these needs and answer prayers. Prayers for healing and miraculous intervention should be encouraged. Use oil to anoint those who are ill. This segment of the faith team meeting can also be used to plan outreach events and programs. Missions and service projects should also be considered.

Kuandaa Church Planting Plan

1. Communicate the church planting vision
    a. Share the vision with pastors in Uganda
    b. Share the vision with pastors, leaders and congregations in the USA

2. Recruit Church Planters and Pastors
    a. Each training event will include one session focused on church planting and evangelism
        i. Emphasizes Great Commission and Great Commandment
    b. Each training event will call for a commitment to evangelism and church planting
        i. "altar call" at close of evangelism session

3. Identify potential pastor/planters
    a. Develop a screening and application process
    b. Pray with pastors/planters for discernment and direction

4. Invite pastor/planters to an orientation session

5. Orientation session at each training event beginning in 2015
    a. Reviews the basic requirements of being a Kuandaa church
    b. Agrees to the responsibilities and commitments
    c. Supports the mission of Kuandaa
    d. Covers the first steps to planting a Kuandaa congregation

6. Each pastor/ planter will develop a three-month, six-month and one year plan for church health, growth and new church planting

Kuandaa Church Planting Covenant

In light of the mission to evangelize the world, and in consideration of Kuandaa International's commitment to train pastors and plant churches, we offer the following proposal. Each church planter/ pastor will be asked to agree to the following covenant with the leadership of Kuandaa International anticipating the presence and blessing of God.

Kuandaa commits to:
- Prayer support for each pastor and congregation
- A mentoring relationship with each pastor
- Unlimited access to all Kuandaa materials
- Weekly communications with Kuandaa mentors (when possible)
- Regular support and advice in ministry matters
- Limited financial support when possible and appropriate
- Kick-off worship service support and cooperation
- Visits and training from Kuandaa International leadership teams

The Pastor/Planter agrees to:
- Scout and identify a location for the new congregation
- Develop a plan for the new church
  - When will worship occur?
  - How will we invite people?
  - Where do we meet?
- Attend all Kuandaa training events
- Attend Kuandaa pastor/planter events
- Maintain regular and meaningful communication with Kuandaa leadership in Uganda and the US

- Maintain accountability in all moral, financial and church-related matters
- Demonstrate a commitment to and progress toward
  - Outreach events
  - Spiritual growth
  - Healthy church practices
  - Educational and Theological pursuits

Part Five: Introduction to Church Planting

Church Planting I
Introduction

If it is true- and I believe it is- that we are commanded by none other than Jesus himself to do the work of evangelism, then we must be about making disciples. And if it is true that church planting is currently the most effective means of doing evangelism- and this is most likely also true- then we who are already disciples should be making every effort to duplicate ourselves and our congregations. The work of evangelism is too important to take it for granted. Church planting is too crucial for us to leave it to chance.

We must be intentionally preaching the gospel, making disciples and starting churches. With or without a comprehensive and coherent strategy, we must at the very least be mindful of the need to do this work.

Too often we have assumed that someone else will do it. After all, they are better trained, closer geographically and socially to those who need the message than we are. The church has made excuses for why she does not do this work for too long. We know that the fields are "white unto harvest," but we have so far been generally unwilling to get involved with the difficult and risky work of joining God in the ministry of evangelism and church planting.

This must change. And it must change now.

Every individual who does not hear the gospel, every man, woman and child who does not turn to Christ is another who does not have access to grace, peace and the assurance of eternal life. Every community without a life giving church is another place where the values of this world reign. This is not the will of God for his creation.

What follows is in part an exhortation for all of us who call on the name of Jesus to get involved. We need to tell others about Christ. Each of us must share responsibility.

It is part instruction manual. Much of what follows is borrowed from Dave Garrison who has written the textbook on Church Planting Movements. There are other sources that will be cited as we move along in this process, as well. We are not interested in reinventing the wheel. Let's learn what we can from those with experience and information and follow them in this great work.

This is also a "permission granting" document. For all of history God has been calling people to follow him and to do his will. There have been people who were called to evangelize and plant churches. We should have the same expectation of God today. There are men and women who long to tell others about the joys that can be found through faith in Christ. If you fit into that category, if you want to do a "new thing" for God, let this be a motivating resource. You now have permission to do the work that God wants you to do. You should feel encouraged and empowered to fulfill the passion that God has put in your heart.

And now one word of qualification. Too often we are laboring under an antiquated idea of 'church.' A church does not have to meet in a building only on Sundays. Church can happen in homes, in workplaces and schools. The church that God is calling you to plant, and then pastor, may consist of seven people who meet only to pray for and encourage one another.

Don't let an artificial definition of church, or evangelism, keep you from doing God's work.

I recently had a conversation with a pastor friend who is very involved in supporting church planting around the world. He has traveled to new churches to encourage them. He and his church have provided financial and material resources to churches and church planting missions organizations. No one questions his commitment to the church and the work of evangelism and church planting.

As he was telling me about his most recent trip overseas to plant churches, and as he shared his vision for future church plants and work supporting and encouraging new congregations, he said to me, "I felt God asking me a hard question. 'If you can go all around the world planting churches, why aren't you doing that close to home?'"

And that is the question for us. "Why aren't we doing this work?"

Church Planting II
Extraordinary Prayer

There is a fine line between ordinary and extraordinary prayer. And both are essential in any work of evangelism or church planting. In fact, it is said that Billy Graham, the famous American evangelist, believes that the three most important things in evangelism are prayer, prayer and prayer.

I don't intend to give a full primer on the basics of prayer here. Suffice it to say that whatever your practice in prayer right now must be continued and increased. We will never be effective in reaching others until we practice prayer.

Let me give you two basic instructions.

1. **In prayer you must spend time with God**. There are no shortcuts. You must devote your energy, attention and devotion to Christ. And you cannot do any of those things without investing time. There is not a minimum time limit that you must get to. There is not a time card that we must punch. As a general challenge, average your current daily prayer time and add to it. I would suggest that you increase your time commitment in prayer by 10% each month. That means that if you prayer for 10 minutes each day, begin praying for 11 minutes at the start of next month.
2. **Develop a relationship with God**. Prayer should never be an obligatory reading of wishes and needs. Prayer is about getting to know the Lord and allowing him to get to know you.

That helps us to get a handle on ordinary prayer. But church planting- successful, God-honoring church planting requires something more of us.

- **Extraordinary prayer is extraordinary in focus.** The thing that we need to be praying for is that God would raise up workers for the harvest (Luke 10.2). We should pray for the hearts of the lost to be softened to the message of Christ. And we need to pray that Jesus would be glorified as people come to faith.
- **Extraordinary prayer is extraordinary in commitment.** This work of evangelism and church planting is the most important thing that we can do. This needs to be the primary focus in our lives. That means that although your discipline of ordinary prayer should be consistent, this prayer is not limited to any time or any particular place. This is an all-encompassing effort.
- **Extraordinary prayer is extraordinary in fellowship.** This is a prayer need that is greater than your ability to handle alone. You should not be doing this on your own. There is a place for private prayer, but you need to enlist a fellowship, a community of pray-ers to join you. Prayer for church planting is a community responsibility.
- **Extraordinary prayer is extraordinary in humility.** It is easy to establish that God is in favor of evangelism. It is not a stretch to believe that he wants the lost to be found, the hurting to be saved. It is also not hard for me to recognize that I cannot do the work of reaching the world by myself. Only God can change a life, restore a family, build a church or forgive sins. I need to be praying that he will be helping me do just that.

Are you ready for some serious encouragement? Here is what the Bible says. "The prayer of a righteous person is powerful and effective." (James 5.16)

Prayer for your church planting program is not only important, it is imperative. Prayer for your new church needs to be regular, simple and extraordinary.

Church Planting III
Abundant Evangelism

The purpose for starting a new congregation is not to rearrange those who already serve God into new groupings. Planting churches is not a ministry for the saved, those already in the church, but for the unchurched. This means that one fundamental aspect of starting a new church is the work of evangelism. We have previously written on this topic and so we will not dwell on it here, but we do need to cover some fundamental issues, especially as they apply to work in new churches.

There is a principle in the Scriptures that can paraphrased as *'if you want a little, ask for a little.'* 1 Corinthians 9.6 reminds us that often we do not have what we need because we have failed to ask. Ephesians 3.20 promises that God can do more than we could ever ask or imagine. It follows, then, that if we want to do a new thing for God, if we want to do the work of an evangelist, if we long for souls to be saved and the church to be built, we must ask for a lot. We need to plant a lot of seeds, build a lot of relationships and always be reaching out.

Many people struggle with evangelism. They are intimidated by those who do not believe. They are afraid of offending someone. Or they are concerned that they might make a mistake while presenting the gospel.

Let me put your mind at ease on that last concern first. You will make mistakes. You will say the wrong thing sometimes and you will hurt someone's feelings. But those things should never keep you from doing evangelism. In fact, your new church will never exist if you do not do this important work. So be bold. Be fearless. Be prepared for the mistakes you will make. And get to work.

In your evangelism, focus on testimonies, personal stories and Biblical parables and illustrations. From time immemorial humans have been moved by stories. They do not need to be tragic, dramatic or funny. Your stories just need to be true. Learn to share your story in a way that will be relatable and simple. And invite people to follow Jesus just as you have.

Remember that Jesus said he came to earth to "seek and to save the lost." (Luke 19.10) This should remind us that those who are lost will not seek us. They are not going to mysteriously show up at your new worship service. We must go find them. That is what Jesus did after all.

Finally, let's approach this endeavor with the idea that we will plant the gospel in our world. If we plant the gospel, the church will spring from it and flourish. As we are sharing our stories and planting our seeds, we should keep in mind that it is God who gives the increase. Let us commit ourselves to planting the gospel everywhere we go.

Church Planting IV
Intentionally On Purpose

There are very few things in life that happen accidentally. In fact, as Christians we believe that there are no coincidences. There is a reason behind everything. This means that everything we do, every project we undertake, even each individual aspect of each project should be bathed in prayer, thoroughly planned and focused on the desired outcome.

Our church planting project is no different. There is nothing of lasting value that comes from lackadaisical planning and haphazard execution. And since we want our church to endure many decades (centuries?) into the future, we must be intentional and purposeful at each point.

Since we believe that we need to be intentional, let's think about what our intentions are.

- **Evangelism is the heartbeat of the gospel.** The Great Commission (Matthew 28.19; Mark 16.15; Acts 1.8) begins the story for us. The church must be concerned for reaching the lost. Every disciple of Jesus Christ needs to be constantly looking for opportunities to share their faith. We are to have as our top priority spreading the gospel to those who have not heard and convincing those who have not believed.
- **There is a plan for developing, planting and building up new churches**. Churches do not just appear. There has to be strategy, planning and prayer in advance. Unfortunately, in many cases a big part of the plan for planting new churches includes raising funds. It is sometimes very expensive to begin a new work.

Wishful thinking will not fulfill the gospel. Nor will dreaming about what might be make it a reality.

- **New churches should be focused on evangelism, discipleship and church planting.** We can never assume that when a new church is established its work is complete. Just because it is viable with members, worship and maybe even property it does not follow that it is finished. The work of the gospel, the task of spreading the word to every tribe and nation, will not be completed until Jesus comes back. Your new church needs to begin planning for the first church it will plant immediately. The message that we have is too important for us to keep it to ourselves.

Start making your plans now. Let the Holy Spirit lead you, but do not neglect researching your community and the people you want to reach. Find the location you will meet. Begin to recruit leaders and church members. And once you have identified your mission and developed your plan, get to work.

Finally, it is important from the beginning to instill in your people the imperative of doing evangelism. A key to this plan is making sure that the identity of church is compatible with a future that includes evangelism and church planting. In too many existing churches we find that outreach, mission and evangelism are foreign concepts. That should never be in any church. Be certain from the start that it is not the case in yours.

Church Planting V
Bible Based

Anyone who has spent any time in the average Christian church in recent days knows that there is a real problem with the Bible. The Bible is fine. We just don't know anything about it. And that is exactly the problem. (This is especially true in American churches, but that is a topic for another time.)

Here are our biblical problems as I see them.

1. The people in the pews do not know the Bible. They don't read it. They don't understand it. And honestly, they are not interested in it. They are essentially biblically illiterate.
2. Our pastors don't teach the Bible or preach from it. They are focusing on current events, or staying relevant, or even the next trendy series.
3. Finally, there are a whole groups of preachers and teachers who misuse and misinterpret the Bible. This is a great tragedy, but what makes this even worse is that there are some Christian leaders who misuse God's word purposely and for their own gain.

Something has to change. A new church plant is the perfect place to begin addressing some of these issues. When we start the work with a foundation built on the Bible and biblical principles, it will be much easier to maintain that going forward. So begin with the Bible.

- **Study the Bible.** A small Bible study group is the perfect place to begin building your church. You will be able to develop relationships and set the precedent of biblical priority. In your new church make sure that a place is given at every meeting for reading and study of God's word. Make it a personal ambition to study the Bible daily. Encourage everyone in your congregation to do the same. Read, study and teach the whole Bible. I have made it a personal mission to read the Bible in its entirety each year. You may want to do the same thing. Memorize Scriptures and make that a goal in your church. Every Christian should have the word of God in his/her heart.

- **Develop a plan for reading and teaching the Bible to your congregation.** The Revised Common Lectionary is one resource that provides a calendar for preaching the whole Bible over a three year period. I challenge my congregation to read the Bible as a group. At the beginning of each year I provide members with a schedule for reading passages. As we learned in the last lesson, we must be intentional about teaching the Bible.
- **Consider the way you read, teach and preach the Bible.** Traditionally, churches have focused on a lecture method for teaching the Bible. We teach and preach in this way. However, the human mind needs more than that. And the Bible is a great resource that lends itself to multiple teaching methods.
    - o Music is one way to teach the Bible. There are hundreds (maybe thousands?) of songs that have been written to be sung to Bible verses. In fact, I recently taught the children in my church the Fruit of the Spirit by helping them learn a song.
    - o Video is another great Bible teaching resource. There are so many videos available that dramatize biblical truths. A few minutes searching online will easily lead you to

hundreds of Christian teachers who offer great video (and audio) teaching resources.

o <u>Storytelling is maybe the most under-used resource I know of</u>. The whole Bible is one epic, beautiful story. Instead of lecturing about the Bible, or preaching about the Bible, try telling some stories from the Bible.

All new churches should be committed to the truth of God's word from the very beginning. We should place a high value on it and expect that to be shared by all those who are a part of our movement. Begin by setting an example for those around you.

Love the Bible. Study the Bible. Teach the Bible.

Church Planting VI
Local Leadership

There is very little to be gained for the Kingdom of God by building empires. We have learned in history, especially recently, that conquering another land and imposing foreign beliefs and practices is completely ineffective, and often counter-productive. Because this is always true, we must look to the practice of placing local pastors and leaders in charge of our new churches. There are several reasons for this.

- **Local leaders are socially acceptable to the community**. There is no learning curve or awkward transition phase. The pastor of your church- it may be you- should be a member of the community that he is intending to serve. She should be aware of the values of his neighbors and church members. She needs to be concerned with the things that others are concerned with. He should love the people that he needs to serve and behave in a way that they can love him as well.
- **Local leaders need a specific conversion and call.** It is not enough for pastors to be good people. Each church leader- new church plants and existing churches alike- need to be able to identify and communicate the story of their conversion. How did you come to faith in Christ? But the second part of this is almost as important. Pastoring a church cannot ever be a career choice. Leaders need to have a distinct sense of being called to the work. This can take many forms, but the pastor-leader of a new congregation needs to know that God has chosen him/her to lead God's people.
- **Local leaders must be able to overcome opposition and adversity.** Starting a new thing is much more

difficult than growing, or even maintaining a current church. There will be practical, legal and spiritual obstacles all along the way. The pastor must be so committed to the work of the local church that she can overcome all of the attacks of the enemy and work through the bouts of discouragement and depression that are likely to follow.

- **Local leaders need have no formal ministry education.** Extensive requirements for ordination and ministry licensure often serve to discourage anointed and called pastors from opting to serve in ministry settings. Finding appropriate ministry candidates need be no harder than determining a person's conversion and Christian commitment, call to ministry and tendency to grow as a disciple of Jesus Christ. Integrity of character and a mentoring relationship with a senior ministry partner should be the only educational requirements for interested participants. It is important to remember that in the first century church, the church of the Apostles, that "being with Jesus" was always more important than academic credentials.

- **Local leaders receive accountability and support from other pastors**. In ministry there can be no lone rangers. Just as the Christian church can only function in community with one another, pastors and other church leaders need the accountability, support and teaching that comes from the collegiality of the company of preachers.

- **Local leaders will preach for response.** All churches, especially new and growing ones, should be characterized by leaders who encourage and call for life change. Pastors should not back away from a message of repentance and salvation. We should always be mindful that Jesus is the only way to God (John 14.6). Our message must be clear and compelling. All people need a relationship with Jesus Christ and those who already have that relationship must be growing closer to him.

Local leaders know the language and traditions of the people they serve. Their familiarity in their setting will always make them more effective. In starting a new congregation look for your pastors and leaders from among the people you plan to reach.

Church Planting VII
Local Leadership, part 2

It is inevitable that there will be problems with local pastors and leaders. This is to be expected. Any time that we have leaders who are inexperienced and untrained we run the risk of mistakes being made. I believe that the risks are worth it, however. The energy, excitement and enthusiasm that young and motivated leaders bring to the church far outweighs the potential damage.

The Apostle Paul believed this to be true, anyway. His practice was to move to a new community, preach the gospel, make converts, plant a church and then move to the next town leaving one of the new converts in charge of the new congregation. Much of the content of Paul's letters deals with training and encouraging those very same pastors. Unfortunately, a lot of the material deals with some of the problems that these men- usually young in age and always young in experience- had encountered and also created.

- o **Teaching problems**- Heresy was a very real problem for the first century church. There were misunderstandings about belief and practice. Around every corner there was a crisis of faith. People who were not experts in doctrine and theology were teaching others, who then often compounded the problem by unintentionally misleading others. This seems like a terrible situation, but it was not so bad that Paul would change his practice or replace poor pastors. Paul's procedure was to correct and rebuke the offending pastor, instruct him on proper doctrine and exhort him to improve. We can expect some disagreements and dissensions, but we should not change our approach too quickly.

o **Moral problems-** Lying, cheating and stealing can easily be great temptations for new pastors in new congregations. It is not uncommon to hear about a leader taking funds from the church offering, or having an adulterous relationship with a church member. These are tragic events and must be addressed, but they are not cause to give up the new church, abandon the work or automatically replace the leader. Consider first that it may be appropriate to offer closer supervision, spiritual restoration and a mentoring relationship. The work that we have to do is too great to let one unwise leader derail it.

o **Practical problems-** Finally, there are many practical or structural problems with new churches. To begin with communication can be very difficult. You must find a way to communicate among the leaders of the congregations on a regular basis. The problems of heresy and moral failure will be diminished if there is a regular interchange between pastor and overseer. Additionally, there may be conflict concerning the organizational structure of the church. Especially with new pastors you may find that they are ill- equipped to lead a Christian organization like a church. Be patient. Offer wise counsel.

All of these are similar to problems in the New Testament. But Paul never gave up. He kept starting congregations and putting new believers in charge of them. Don't forget that it is the new believer who has a passion for his faith and to have his friends and family come to faith. It is also the new believer who has the most unsaved friends and acquaintances. Let's put them to work in this role that seems too complicated to us, but can be a great blessing to God and the gospel message.

Church Planting VIII
Single Cell Churches

It is my conviction that evangelism is imperative. I also believe that church planting is the most effective way of doing evangelism. Furthermore, it seems clear, to me at least, that the single cell church is the easiest church to establish and the most reliable in terms of offering effective and regular pastoral care to church members.

Single cell churches can be called by many names. The ones that are most common, or the ones that I prefer include faith teams, mini- churches, house churches, cells or home groups.

A single cell church is one that is small enough that one pastor or leader can care for all of the pastoral needs of the group, that all members can know one another personally and at a fairly familiar level, and that allows members to have a genuine love and concern for one another and for the Lord. Members challenge one another in matters of faith, and encourage each other in times of trial. They call one another to repentance when a member falls into sin and celebrate victory whenever there is a healing, an accomplishment or an answered prayer.

Generally speaking, a single cell church will consist of 15-50 members, but there are always exceptions to this. Many of these churches will grow beyond 50 congregants with little problem. And it will be that some groups of 8-12 will also constitute a church.

Guiding Principles

- **People are more important than buildings**. This is always true. Although there may come a time that your new church will desire- or even need- a new building, that building can never be more important than the people who occupy it. If the primary value of your church is to build "God people", then you will not lose sight of this important principle.
- **Groups of people are more significant than the traditional church**. How we love our traditions. Our shared history speaks to us in ways that nothing else can. But remember, when you are attempting to reach new people your traditions mean nothing to them. If you have to choose between evangelism and tradition, always pick winning the lost.
- **Relationships lead to evangelism**. There is a place in the church from massive evangelism crusades. We should have rallies and crusades and door to door canvas efforts. We should also use radio, television and print media to spread the word. But in most cases lost people only come to Christ through relationships with people who already know Jesus. We Christians have to be identifying, cultivating and building relationships with lost people. Don't lose sight of this principle.
- **Relationships build churches**. A church is not just a group of people that organize around a common cause. Churches are made up of people who love one another. A church is not a building where random people meet. Churches are made up of people with shared commitments and accountability with one another. Remember, a person who visits your congregation but does not develop a relationship with someone else at church will not stay for long.

Church Planting IX
Church Planting and Evangelism DNA

One key factor for your new church must be to consider the philosophy of its existence. Just as your body has DNA that dictates what you look like and who you are, your church will have a particular DNA as well. It is important that you, the pastor, implant the appropriate mission in your congregation from the very beginning.

<u>Guiding Principles</u>

- **Evangelism should be the expectation of every group.** Since Jesus commanded the church to make disciples and to do evangelism we must do that work. It is not enough to pay lip service to reaching out. The church must be expected to always be reaching out. The lost will not be coming to you. You must go to those who still need to know Jesus. From the very beginning you must teach and model evangelism.
- **Plans should develop early on for multiplying.** From the very beginning you need to develop plans not only to evangelize in your community, but to begin other churches. Build the expectation in your members that you will be building the church by multiplying congregations.
- **Leaders should always be identifying potential new leaders.** If the church is going to multiply, if there are going to be new churches, then we will need new leaders. Those who are leading God's people must always be on the lookout for the next evangelist, the next pastor, the next leader. Find people who are gifted and willing to serve in ministry. You may not have to

wait too long. The next church planter may already be in your new church community.

- **Groups should always be preparing for new groups.** One of the hardest parts of planting new churches is separation. Individuals within your church will build relationships with one another. Accountability will develop and men and women will become attached. There will be a tendency to love the community so much that the church will resist separation when the time for it comes. Don't allow this to distract or deter you! From the very beginning of your church's existence prepare for the time when a team is sent out to start a new congregation.

Church Planting X
Rapid Reproduction

Complacency is a significant danger for any church. This seems to be especially true of church plants. A young congregation has several hurdles to overcome. They need to get off the ground by beginning to have regular meetings and worship services. They need to become viable as churches, with a sense or consistency in meeting, attendance, structure and benefit to members. And when these things are accomplished, new churches can easily slip into a season of risk avoidance.

That is, an attitude that protects the status quo can creep in unintentionally and even unnoticed. We love what we have and so we do not want to take chances. We avoid making decisions that might rock the boat. Churches can easily come to avoid all changes. After all, if I love the way things are now, why would I want anything different to happen?

Although this is a common and somewhat understandable approach, we must avoid it. In fact, we must move toward multiple changes in quick succession, all the time. This, we will find, leads to rapid reproduction of disciples and congregations.

For this to happen, however, we must:

- **Overcome our fear of failure**. It is the natural tendency of every human to long for success. We are selfish and competitive by nature. But for true success to take place we must be willing to fail sometimes.

- **Overcome our reluctance to change**. It is easy to comfortable in our beliefs, our understanding of the world and our habits and actions. Change is hard and a little bit scary. But none of the great advances in human history would have ever taken place without people who were willing to change.
- **Overcome our aversion to quick and decisive action**. Q: How many Christians does it take to change a lightbulb? A: Seven. One to screw it in and six to make sure that it doesn't hurt anyone's feelings. Sometimes we just have to do what needs to be done. Make a decision and take a stand, for crying out loud!
- **Allow God to fill us with faith.** There are times that we will find making changes to be impossible. We will lack the direction or the confidence to do what needs to be done. That is when we need God to take over and do the work through us.
- **Be open to hearing and following God's will.** Listen to God. It isn't always easy, but it is always beneficial. Get his direction and get on board.

All of this leads us to the idea of rapid reproduction. Your new church should start another new congregation as soon as possible. And then that new church should plant a new church while your original church is planning and working toward starting another one. The larger church will grow exponentially when we can make this happen in conjunction with God's leading.

Church Planting XI
Healthy Churches

After we are certain that we are planting churches and winning the lost, we need to ensure that the churches we plant are healthy. There are many tools in the world to evaluate health and effectiveness of the church. You can find assessments and other resources to help you measure your local church's health and help you to take steps to improve that health. Find one that will work for you and your situation and use it. Colossians 3.17 reminds that everything we do should be for God's glory. A church should definitely fit into this category.

To help you start on the right foot, I suggest that you practice and teach the "4 Most Important Things".

- **Bible study.** We have already covered the importance of Scripture for the new church. Be sure that this is true for the individual Christian and his spiritual growth as well. Make sure that you believe and teach the Bible and do all in your power to get your church members to place a high value on God's Word as well. *Healthy churches are Bible reading churches.*
- **Prayer.** As we discussed earlier, you can do nothing of value in the church or in the world without prayer. Teach your congregation to pray. Lead them in prayer. Build a praying church. *Healthy churches are praying churches.*
- **Fellowship.** Again, this is a topic that we have covered before. A healthy church is one that not only worships together, but also makes room for social times. There will be those occasions when your people will support one another emotionally and spiritually simply by being

present with one another. *Healthy churches are churches that fellowship together.*

- **Ministry.** Finally, a ministry-focused philosophy is essential in a healthy church. This includes the focus on evangelism that we previously discussed, but we need to also participate in other forms of ministry as well. Be caring for the sick and elderly, the orphan, the homeless and the hopeless. Develop outreach opportunities in every direction. *Healthy churches are ministry-focused churches.*

I recently read a little story that seems perfect at this point. This illustration will help you understand what it means to be a healthy congregation. You see, frogs move slowly and sit in one place for long periods of time. They wait around for the flies to come to them. And then when a fly comes close enough, the frog will quickly strike with its tongue, capture and eat the insect. They get to eat, but they don't get much exercise. Sadly, the frog becomes fat and lazy. And this is the situation with many churches. We want new people to come to our churches, but we wait around for them to arrive. Consequently, real ministry to the unchurched is infrequent and haphazard.

There is another animal that lives on flies, however. Lizards are always on the move. They are constantly in pursuit of their next meal. They travel in difficult places like up walls and into cracks. Lizards are not lazy and generally do not get fat. Our churches should be more like lizards, always looking for the next one we can reach. We should be constantly on the move, exercising our faith and not waiting for the needs to come to us. We must be looking for the needs that God is calling us to meet.

Church Planting XII
Discipleship Focus

We have spent a lot of time and energy on evangelism and converting the lost- and rightfully so. Without this important work the church would not grow and within one generation would cease to exist entirely. We cannot overlook evangelism, ever. But at the same time, we cannot assume that the work of the church ends when a person receives Christ as his Savior. There must be a discipleship focus that works toward assimilating new Christians into the life of the church and building them up in their spiritual lives.

There are many churches that focus so much on evangelism and large outreach events that they completely neglect the spiritual lives of those who have come to faith. The work of big event outreach evangelism is important, but without a planned focus on discipleship, the gains to the kingdom in new converts will be lost as they are not fully incorporated into the life of the church.

There needs to be a two-step process at play in every church.

- **Assimilation.** Those who visit our churches should be quickly surrounded with the love and care of the congregation. New persons should be included in social settings, educational opportunities and leadership positions. Keep track of new people and put them to work. Turn visitors into workers, workers into leaders and leaders into church planters.
- **Discipleship.** We must be intentional about helping our people to grow spiritually. Once they have met Jesus, get them quickly acquainted with the spiritual

disciplines that will help them grow in faith. Be sure to emphasize the *4 Most Important Things* and get your people doing that as soon as possible.

All of this is just common sense for any thoughtful leader in the church. However, just because we know we ought to be doing these things doesn't mean that we are, or that we will. There must be specific steps in place to accomplish this process. Remember the old cliché (it turns out to be true): "If you fail to plan, you plan to fail." Make sure that you plan to succeed with the discipleship and spiritual growth of your congregation.

Church Planting XIII
Passionate, Indigenous Worship

The best place to begin this discussion of worship in your new church is with a definition of worship. There is a lot of controversy surrounding this topic, but at its very essence we can say that worship is simply being with God. There is not a certain requirement for time, or location, or even musical style. The bottom line is that worship is anytime that we encounter God in a real way.

With that being said, and without putting too much emphasis on specifics, let's consider the following components of a worship service. Each of these should be present in each worship service.

- **Praise**. Regardless of the music (or lack of music), each worship service must be characterized by praise for God. It is, after all, a service of worship. Offer thanks and praise to God, no matter what else you do or do not do.
- **Bible.** There should always be a message or study from the Scriptures. This could be a lesson, a discussion, a sermon, or a group of people reading the Bible together, but every service needs to be focused on God's Word.
- **Prayer.** Prayer is a sure sign of being in the presence of God. There should be prayer of worship, prayers of intercession and prayers of commitment.
- **Service/ Ministry.** In our services we ought to be helping one another and others. This can manifest itself in prayer times, teaching times, or opportunities to care for the needs of those outside your church.

- **Fellowship.** Community is a large part of the church. We are the body of Christ and we need each other. There should be a definite social aspect to what the church is doing and what it stands for.

General Guidelines:
- **Every church must be culturally relevant.** There can never be any sort of imperial influence from an outside agency, congregation or person. The church will only be effective in reaching its specific community as it speaks to the individuals and groups within it.
    o The church must worship in its native language. This is not only a linguistic concern, but also cultural one. You cannot reach street people with an Ivy League vocabulary. Use the words of the people that you are targeting.
    o Music must also be appropriate for the location. Inner city urban areas are not good places to use southern gospel music. Likewise, you cannot reach the rural south of the US by worshiping with hip-hop music.
    o Expectations must be realistic. That is to say, a suburban American mega-church will not grow, or even survive, in a rural African village. Make sure that the church you want and plan for is consistent with what is reasonable and what God is calling you to do.
- **The location of your church is important, but don't get hung up on the building.** Churches can exist in houses, shops, fields or even under a tree. Your church needs to be where the people are, but it doesn't have to have pews and a steeple.

- **Finally, your church needs to be a community of equals.** There does need to be a pastor/teacher, but you want to be sure that what you create is not a hierarchical system of leadership. Always remember that Jesus was the leader of the disciples, but he said he came to serve. Don't make your leadership an authoritarian ploy to gain power.

Church Planting XIV
Sacrifice and Suffering

Let there be no misunderstanding. Ministry is difficult. Evangelism and church planting are even harder. There will be discouragements and disappointments at every turn. People will come to faith in Christ, become an important part of your congregation and then turn away from discipleship. You will get your feelings hurt. And that is on a good day.

You should know from the beginning that there will be opposition to what God has called you to do. The enemy does not want the kingdom advancing. Ever. There will be family members and loved ones who will try to persuade you to give up this dream of building the church. Community leaders will come against you. Other religious leaders- Christian and otherwise- will mount attacks. Be prepared.

Remember that we are called to be faithful. We are to follow Jesus and his calling regardless of the consequences. Do what God has called you to do. No matter what.

There will be opposition. There will persecution. There will be suffering and sacrifice. This is all part of the battle that we are engaged in. Never forget that in all of this conflict we are not alone. Jesus will never leave us. He will encourage and strengthen us. All we have to do is turn to him.

Our God is greater than any adversity. He is bigger than any opponent that presents itself. God will supply all our needs.

One final caution: It can become very easy to focus so much on our difficulties that we lose sight of God's goodness and grace. Never let that happen. Be filled with the Holy Spirit and let him rule in your life. Troubles will come, but we are more than conquerors through him who loves us (Romans 8.37).

Church Planting XV
Passion for the Mission

A final characteristic of successful church planting and church planting movements is that those involved in church planting are filled with passion for the mission to which they are called. In fact, we could say that passion is a key element of any and all successful, God-honoring ministry.

One significant problem that many church leaders face is that they are not called to ministry. There are some who have made ministry a career choice, rather than a faithful response to God's call. They consider the professional perks- financial and otherwise- as well as the respect and status that pastoring sometimes brings and mistakenly believe that it is a logical professional path. In this way of thinking, ministry is viewed simply as one option in a world of many. You can decide between being a doctor, a merchant, or a pastor. This should never be, though.

- **Those who are planting and leading churches must first of all, have a a passion for God and his ways.** Your relationship with the Lord must be your primary consideration. Get to know Jesus as well as you can. Be as faithful to him as possible. Follow him closely.
- **Your second passion must be for the call of God on your life.** Not everyone gets the opportunity to do God's work the same way as those who are called. It is an honor to be selected by God to serve him. And the good news is this: Those who are called, and are obedient to that call live an abundant life that is fulfilling to the extreme.

- **Your final passion must be to the work of church planting.** It is a specific call that causes us to devote our lives to evangelism. We must give ourselves entirely to it. You will find yourself working extra hours to reach new people. You will be energized by opportunities to share the gospel. You will spend more time at this project than you ever planned to, and find that there is still more to do.

There is no substitute for passion in ministry. If you are not already energized about your relationship with God, your call to serve him, or the work that you are doing, begin to pray that God will fill you with that passion now. Pray that God will fill you with a love for the lost and a desire to see his kingdom grow.

Church Planting XVI
The Last Word (for now)

If there were to be a last word- and I am not sure there never really can be a final word- about church planting, it should be about measuring success. After all, we should establish from the outset what we intend to accomplish and how we will know when we have accomplished it. There are many standards by which evaluations are made, but ours will be very specific. In fact, we will look at four criteria by which we will determine the effectiveness and success of any and all church plants.

- **Our new churches will be self-governed.** Although there will be advice offered from outside, and some oversight will be required, at least initially, it is important for the long term sustainability of the church that it make its own decisions. This means that leadership will come from within and the church planting agency, denomination, mission organization or apostolic figure will release governance of the church to the church and its members.
- **Our new churches will be self-supporting.** A relationship that causes a "church" to be dependent on the resources of someone outside of its self is never a healthy situation. In fact, I maintain that if leadership and financing are coming from outside the congregation the resulting entity is not a church at all. The members of the local church need to- as quickly as possible- take responsibility for the church in every way.
- **Our new churches will be self-replicating.** The church that does not begin its life making plans to start more new churches is doomed to a history of stagnation. There will be periods of growth- numerical

and spiritual- but the life-giving power that comes from the evangelistic work of Christ empowered by the Holy Spirit will never know its fullest potential. Therefore, it is imperative that we begin our life as a congregation with a commitment to create more congregations. Make plans to start more churches even as you are planning to start the first one.

- **Our new churches will be self-contained.** There is no need for outside curriculum or programming. We can avoid peripheral teachings and events. We do not need the support of government, community or social entities. Our churches will be complete unto themselves.

Church Planting Appendix
Scriptural Background

Church planting is an important ministry of the church and as such, we can find instruction and encouragement for this important ministry in the words of the Bible, particularly through the teachings of Jesus himself.

<u>Matthew 10</u>

*And as you go, preach, saying, 'The kingdom of heaven is at hand.' **Verse 7***

Preaching, witnessing, sharing your faith should be a regular part of your life. You should be telling others about Jesus as go about your daily activities. This is consistent with Jesus' words in Acts 1.8. "You shall be witnesses." This is something that should happen, must happen, and in a perfect situation, witnessing automatically happens.

*Heal the sick, cleanse the lepers, raise the dead, cast out demons. **Verse 8***

There are seasons of excitement, activity and success in the work to which Jesus has called us. At these times ministry seems like a joy to us. It is something that we love doing and we are energized by it. But sometimes we must do work. We are called to do the work of ministry. We are given gifts to help us accomplish this, but we must always be willing to get going, even when it is not as fun or fulfilling.

*Provide neither gold nor silver nor copper in your money belts, nor bag for your journey, nor two tunics, nor sandals, nor staffs; for a worker is worthy of his food. **Verses 9-10***

We previously discussed how important it is to view ministry as a calling rather than a career. This is emphasized here. Do not expect wealth, fame or popularity. We must always be focused on simplifying our lives. Effective ministry requires that we are not burdened with too much stuff.

Now whatever city or town you enter, inquire who in it is worthy. **Verse 11**

Focus your efforts on those who are open to the ministry that you have to offer. Find the 'person of peace' who will respond to your message. Once you have a convert, more people will certainly follow. God will lead you to relationships that will glorify him and bring many to faith.

Luke 10

*...the Lord appointed seventy others also, and sent them two by two... **verse 1***

God has put us into community. We are born into families and we worship in congregations. We also see that it is his will that we do ministry together. To that end, find a partner to be in ministry with. This can take a couple of forms:
- **First of all, work with another person to plant a church together.** You can accomplish twice as much, you will always have an advocate to advise you, keep you focused and encourage you as you move forward.
- **Secondly, you can find another pastor/ planter who will share the emotional roller coaster that you are encountering.** Help each other as much as possible.

Pray the Lord of the harvest to send out laborers into His harvest. **Verse 2**

Never forget to pray. Pray for success in your work. Pray for those to whom you are ministering. Pray for co-laborers in the harvest. Pray that the church will be established and grow. Pray a lot. And then pray some more.

Carry neither money bag, knapsack, nor sandals; and greet no one along the road. **Verse 4**

There are a lot of things that can serve to distract us in life and especially in ministry. As we simplify our personal needs we will become less distracted. Focus on what God is calling you to do. Do not be overwhelmed by needs around you, or so focused on other items that you lose sight of what God is calling you to do.

The Great Commission

Go therefore and make disciples of all the nations, baptizing them in the name of the Father and of the Son and of the Holy Spirit, teaching them to observe all things that I have commanded you; and lo, I am with you always, even to the end of the age. **Matthew 28.19-20**

Go into all the world and preach the gospel to every creature. **Mark 16.15**

You shall receive power when the Holy Spirit has come upon you; and you shall be witnesses to Me in Jerusalem, and in all Judea and Samaria, and to the end of the earth. **Acts 1.8**

As I see it, the main theme of all three of these passages is that we need to go. (There are many other things that we should glean from them, such as the importance of discipleship, the need of all people for salvation, being empowered by the Holy Spirit for ministry. For now, however, we will focus on "going" to do ministry.) Too many people want the unsaved to come to our meetings and our churches. We provide buildings, staff and programs so that the lost will come. However, Jesus made it clear that the Christian is to go. This means that we need to go to wherever the gospel is needed. And that is everywhere. We should be sharing the message of Christ with those who will never come to our churches.

That means that we should be starting new churches in new communities. We should be joining groups and organizations that do not have a Christian witness. We are commanded to go!

Part Six: Church Basics
What Makes a Church?

Church Basics 1: Frequency and Consistency

*So continuing daily with one accord in the temple, and breaking bread from house to house... **Acts 2.46***

Let's begin by dealing with the elephant in the room. The very first Christians, the original church, met for worship and teaching every day. Acts 2.46 makes it clear that these early believers were frequent and consistent worshipers. This is an intimidating prospect for the modern believer. We sometimes find it a struggle to commit a few hours to worship on one morning each week.

I am not planning to put pressure on anyone about how often a congregation should gather for worship. Each church should be led by God's will for them. Likewise, every individual Christian must be guided by the will of God and his own conscience. I am not advocating a one size fits all approach to worship, but rather a philosophy that makes gathering with believers for the primary purpose of worshiping God a singular priority. Each believer must deal with God on his own. We must all work out our own salvation with fear and trembling (Philippians 2.12).

As church leaders- pastors and church planters especially- we must be careful to consider the following factors as we begin the process of planning worship, leading the church, and moving into all that God wants us to do.

- **Make sure that there are opportunities for worship.** You will need to gauge the interest and commitment levels of congregation members, but you need to be certain there is a schedule of activities and services for people to participate in. When you have determined when services will be, make sure that you are consistent in providing them. Traditionally, Christian worship services have occurred on Sunday mornings. Many congregations offer studies, prayer groups or other services at various times during the week as well.

- **Make sure that your services are convenient to those who will be attending.** Do not plan a service when a significant number in your congregation will be working or obligated elsewhere. This convenience factor does not only apply to the time and day of worship services, but also to location. We will look at where the church meets later.

- **Make sure that the church service/ worship experience is "normal" for those you are trying to reach.** This is not to say that you should compromise how you do things, but to encourage you to consider how to effectively reach those in your community. You will most likely do this by eliminating obstacles to the comfort and understanding of your people.

- **Make sure that you celebrate those who attend your church.** Too many people and congregations expend a lot of energy encouraging participation through negative reinforcement. Do not make those who miss services feel guilty. Encourage and cheer those who become most faithful.

Another aspect of the worship experience to consider, especially in a new or non-traditional congregation is that worship is primarily an attitude of the Christian believer. I have often said that the basic element of worship is simply being with God. This is unequivocally true. However, let's add that worship is also an attitude. The passage that we are considering reminds us that those Christians in first century Jerusalem were unified. Not only are we to be unified, but our worship should also be marked by joy in our fellowship, our singing, our praying and our teaching.

Finally, remember that the location of your church is less important than you may think. The church in Acts 2 did not meet in a building dedicated to Christian worship. The disciples met in the Jewish Temple, where they were not necessarily welcomed. They met in a public setting where anyone else could meet at any time. At any point they could have been arrested, persecuted and martyred for meeting in that location. They also met in their homes. They did not feel the need to meet in a fancy building. You should expect that at least initially you will need to meet somewhere other than a church building.

- <u>Meet in homes.</u> This is definitely a biblical idea. Someone in your congregation has a home where you can gather with a small group of believers. When you outgrow the house, you can move to the yard where you can find a tree to meet under.
- <u>Be creative and find some other place to meet</u>. Restaurants, school buildings, community centers, store fronts and coffee shops all can provide an inexpensive, convenient place to meet.

Church Basics 2: Structure and Administration

Let's begin with the end: Humans pay attention to structure and administration because they want to be in control of life. But the Christian is called to give God control of every aspect of his being. This paradox is problematic in the church because we want God to be in charge, but we also need to maintain order, orthodoxy and accountability.

To deal with these sticky conflicts we should begin by considering what the New Testament has to say about structure in the church. You might be surprised to find that it doesn't say much at all.

- The pattern that we see most often includes Paul **visiting a community and establishing a congregation**. After a period of time- usually 18-24 months- he picks a new pastor and then moves on to the next town on the map.
- There are occasional **follow up visits from Paul, but essentially, once he has left the community he provides some specific direction for the pastor** (see 1 Timothy, 2 Timothy and Titus, for example). There is little more than that as far as leadership recruitment and pastoral training are concerned.
- **A large portion of Paul's general letters to the churches consist of his efforts to deal with heresy and aberrant practices that have come up.** This is the complete effort at supervision that Paul puts in place.

It seems as though Paul realized the assertion at the beginning of this lesson. He knew that God needed to be in control. Because of that, Paul did not establish a denomination in any way.

Paul understood what we need to come to grips with. Leadership comes from God. The church and its leaders should be getting direction primarily from God, not an overseer, bishop, superintendent or denomination. We must answer to God first, last and always.

There is the potential for false teaching, however. It is possible that heresy will creep into your congregation. This is where the community at large comes into play. If the church as a whole is studious in the word of God, vigilant about its faith and history, then it will serve as the protector of the integrity of the church itself. Remember that the gospel doesn't need is to defend it. We do need to make sure that the church is faithful at all times.

All of this leads us to one conclusion. We must not be consumed by rules, organizational structure, laws and administrative concerns. The bottom line for us is that we must find a balance between keeping our church(es) organized enough to maximize our gospel potential, and responsive enough to God's voice that we are able to follow him at all times and at any cost. What the basic church needs is to be obedient to God above all else.

Church Basics 3: Oversight and Association

*...and that day about three thousand souls were added to them. **Acts 2.41***

After we have considered the pitfalls of structure, rules and administration in the governing of any church- but especially a new church- let's consider the ways in which structure is not only beneficial, but necessary to a congregation. The two areas that are most essential are oversight and association.

<u>Oversight</u>

Every church, whether in a denomination or not, needs some oversight. This should never be construed as a dictatorial leader who requires adherence to practices or beliefs. There should be an overseer for every church which is separate from the congregation. This overseer could relate to, or pastor a church, and may have responsibility for the oversight of several congregations. It is crucial that she/he is a faithful disciple, a godly leader and a gifted follower of Jesus. The primary foci of responsibility for this overseer are as follows:

- **The overseer is charged with supporting and encouraging the pastors and churches** for which he/she has responsibility. The overseer should be familiar with the individuals and churches for whom she serves. The overseer should regularly offer prayers and messages of inspiration.
- **The overseer is charged with training the leaders of the churches and community and providing training opportunities** for members of the congregations.

Overseers should always be looking to recruit, train and deploy new leaders and pastors.

- **The overseer is charged with coordinating the activities and ethos of the church association.** It is the overseer's responsibility to foster community in the churches and among and between them as well.

Association

All churches, for the sake of their own health and the spiritual Heath of their congregants, should be in association and community with the larger body of Christ. What follows are some of the advantages of this sort of association.

- **Churches should be in association with one another for the sake of fellowship.** It is the will of God for Christians- and congregations- to exist and grow with one another.
- **Churches should be in association with one another for the sake of accountability**. When we are working closely together, supporting one another, and even monitoring each other, we will all be healthier as a result.
- **Churches should be in association with one another for the sake of sharing.** This one is very simple. Our work is much more effective, efficient and meaningful when we share resources and ideas with other congregations.

Church Basics 4: Elements of Worship Fellowship

The next several lessons in this series will try to address the fundamental elements that are essential for all worship services. There are many good things that you may want to incorporate in your worship, and the way you apply these particular elements may vary, but it is necessary that every worship service and event make plans to include these things.

This instruction includes the element of Christian fellowship. This may seem like a topic that does not need attention. But unfortunately, if we are not intentional about each element, they may fall into disuse which will signal the decline and eventual end of the congregation. As you are considering fellowship in your church, think about it in the following ways.

- **Fellowship is a significant way that we build up the body of Christ.** Christian believers need time to be together socially. There is an attitude of support, affinity and accountability that develops among Jesus' followers as we spend time together.
- **Fellowship allows us to express genuine concern for one another.** There is no room for false "niceties", or polite interest. Christians should be loving and concerned for each other. Likewise, we should never allow jealousy, envy or bitterness. These things violate the spirit of fellowship that we are trying to foster.
- **Fellowship encourages us to share good will and God's grace with our brothers and sisters in Christ.** When we are in this sort of Christian relationship we naturally find ourselves rooting for the betterment of others. In fact, we will find that we are advocating for the blessing, advancement and strength of those around

us. And ultimately, this attitude of support and helping works toward the benefit of the whole congregation.

- **Fellowship must be more than a merely social mingling of likeminded people.** It is good that we fellowship and support one another in a physical and emotional way, but there must be a spiritual element as well.

  - We need to follow the pattern of the first Christians who also broke bread together. On the one hand we know that eating together is a significant source of emotional bonding between people. The act of taking a meal together is a mysterious event that allows many psychological, social and emotional barriers to be broken down. In addition, there is a sacramental consideration to breaking bread together. The spiritual significance of Jesus' instructions to partake of his body and blood should never be dismissed. We need to always be in the practice of, and mindful of, the importance of breaking bread in fellowship.

  - Fellowship becomes spiritual when we lift the burdens of one another. Being present in the time of need, praying for healing, consolation or strength, or assisting those who struggle are all ways that we can be in fellowship together. Always be certain to care for the needs of those around you, and especially those in your congregation.

  - Fellowship is spiritual when it encourages, admonishes and instructs others in a spirit of grace and love. Be a positive force in the lives of your friends and neighbors, and especially in the life of your church family.

Church Basics 5: Elements of Worship
Teaching and Preaching

It is not desirable that we should leave the word of God. **Acts 6.2**

The primary tool that the modern Christian has in developing his faith, and ensuring effectiveness in ministry is to pay special attention to the study of the Bible. It is good for our personal, spiritual lives and for our work in the church as well. We need to know God's word for our own edification and for the empowerment of those we are called to serve. To that end, we must keep in mind the importance of teaching the Bible and preaching the Word of God. In fact, every worship service, every public meeting, every gathering of believers should be marked by a time of teaching.

All of this begins with the training and preparation of the church's leaders. You cannot expect that God will miraculously inspire you at the moment of the sermon. It could be that there will be times- rare occasions- when the Holy Spirit will move in your heart, and anoint your words so that you can bring a message extemporaneously. Do not rely on that as a regular course of action, however. The pastor/ preacher must plan for messages in advance. A good practice would be for you to plan your sermon topics around four to six weeks ahead of time. That may change, but it is good to have a schedule to work toward. Then spend time each week studying the passage and the topics that you want to cover. Pray for God to lead you where he wants you to go. To have an effective teaching time, prayer and planning are necessary.

A secondary consideration is to remember that all our teaching should be based on the Bible. If it is in the Bible, we should be teaching it. If it is not a biblical concept, then you should be careful about sharing it with others. It could be good and valuable information, but only what comes from God's word should be the basis for our preaching and teaching.

The topics that you cover, the messages that you preach and the lessons that you teach should all prepare members of your congregation for living a Christian life. Sometimes there will be an occasion when you will teach your people something just for the sake of giving them the information, but ultimately, the work of ministry is designed to move people closer to God. So ask yourself whether or not you are building disciples. Is your teaching doing the work of the gospel?

Another consideration in teaching is to provide inspiration for your congregation and its members to overcome their trials and live a victorious Christian life. There will be times for prophetic words, corrective instruction and rebuking false teachings and beliefs, but we need to always be encouraging the people of God.

Finally, an important part of our teaching needs to include general training in the Bible and how to study it. We should be equipping our people to read and study the Bible on their own. It is imperative that Christians are well versed in God's Word and a part of our job is to give them the tools to do it.

Church Basics 6: Elements of Worship
Praise and Worship

*... praising God and having favor with all the people. And the
Lord added to the church daily those who were being saved.*
Acts 2.47

An unfortunate and inaccurate correlation has taken place in
many churches. There are several pastors and congregations
who equate a discussion of praise and worship with music, or
even a particular style of music. This should not be. Although
music is a great tool for bringing people into the presence of
God, and it is often helpful in creating a worshipful
atmosphere, music is not necessary for the worship of God by
individuals or congregations.

Let's define the act of worship as being in the presence of God.
Fellowship with the Creator, inspired by the filling and the
work of the Holy Spirit, is the essence of worship. With that
understanding we can confidently assert that worship is a
function of the Christian life. Our faith should be characterized
by regular and consistent times of worship. This means that we
are to worship when we are alone in prayer, as well as in the
congregation on Sunday morning. And even though it is true
that worship is a personal and private activity, as well as a
public one, we are going to primarily concern ourselves with
the worship of the gathered congregation. And even though
praise and worship includes much more than this, we will
primarily focus on the purpose and use of music.

Every worship service, or meeting, of the congregation should
be filled with times of praise and worship. It is called a worship
service because the intended purpose of the gathering is to

worship God. Church leaders should use whatever tools are necessary and appropriate to make sure that the congregation does experience the presence of God. The tools we use should always be appropriate to the congregation and the culture, however. For example, some congregations will respond to a choir and formal or classical musical accompaniment. Others will prefer a more contemporary folk or popular music style. For example, your church may want to worship while accompanied by drums, guitars or dancers. In any of these cases take care to make sure that all practices are biblically appropriate and speak to the needs and preferences of the people.

In fact, as far as music is concerned, instruments are not even necessary. They may enhance praise and worship, but people can worship God without accompaniment. In all of these concerns we are mindful that the style of the music, or even the style of the worship, is less important than the attitude of the worshipers. Leaders need to model a heart devoted to worship and encourage that same spirit in others, regardless of personal tastes or preferences.

Church Basics 7: Elements of Worship
Service and Mission

...for the equipping of the saints for the work of ministry...
Ephesians 4.12

The body of Christ does works of service. Do not overlook this fact. This is not a command. We do not read it as if the church must serve. It is not a suggestion. The Scriptures do not teach that it would be a good idea to be missional, or involved in mission work. The simple fact of the matter is that the church, the body of Christ does works of service.

This brief article will not offer suggestions for the types of service and mission that your church should be involved in. You should discern the specific applications based on your community, culture and the leading of God in your life. I will not be giving you guidelines about how often you should serve others, or for how long, or how much money you should spend in missions. All of these concerns should be answered in the context of your community.

For the sake of clarity and ease of discussion, let's make a somewhat arbitrary distinction between service and mission.

- **When we talk about service, we intend for it to mean the ministry that we offer and provide to the congregation at large, and the individual members of the church.** Service is the body of Christ taking care of itself. It is service that allows us to love and carry the burdens of our fellow believers.
- Conversely, **mission is the outreach component of local church ministry.** Mission is taking the gospel

and other caring ministries to those in our communities and around the world who do not know Jesus.

There are a couple of warnings to take into consideration. First of all, all of our works- service and mission- are a response to the grace of God in our lives. We do ministry not because we want God to love and bless us, but we do it because he already has loved and blessed us and we long to share that grace with others. A serious danger in many churches and in the lives of many believers is to somehow come to the belief that doing works of service will somehow get us favor with God. Don't let this be a problem in your life, or in your church.

Secondly, please keep in mind that all service and mission should point to Jesus. It is good to feed the hungry, but we must also tell them about the Lord. We should definitely visit the sick and the prisoner, but while we are visiting we must be sure to pray for them to be drawn closer to Christ.

Finally, every church must intentionally focus on both service and mission. I am not sure how that translate into action in your local setting and in your weekly worship experience. Perhaps there is a time designated for praying for one another, counseling and sharing burdens. It could be that at the close of every service the congregation will disperse into the community to share the Good News. Maybe your church will be meeting in a visible community space. In any case, be sure to do the work that Christ has commanded.

Church Basics 8: Elements of Worship
Prayer

Earlier we defined worship as being in the presence of God. We should think about prayer in much the same way. Prayer does not require a particular physical position, nor are we required say certain things. There is not a form or ritual that prayer must abide by. When we pray we are merely being in communication with our Creator.

There is one distinction that should be made concerning prayer. The personal and private prayer times of the Christian are characterized by- or they should be characterized by- dialogue. A human relationship necessarily consists of two or more people involved in two-way conversation. Keep this in mind as you pray. Do not be so consumed by your needs and requests that you are unable to hear God speaking to you. Listen for his instructions and be obedient to his word.

A corporate worship experience may have to be a little bit different. Since there are multiple people talking to God, listening to his voice could potentially become complicated and confusing. Be patient as you work this out. It will take practice, patience and time, but in the end it will be well worth it.

- **Corporate prayer must include confession of sins.**
  There may not be an opportunity for individuals to confess their sins in a public worship service, but that does not eliminate the necessity for confession. Perhaps members should confess their sins silently during a time of prayer. Maybe a leader will say a 'prayer of confession' that the congregation will respond to. It could be that the Holy Spirit will move in a place in

such a way that a time of testimony and confession is appropriate. In this situation, allow the Spirit to move, but never put anyone under any sort of obligation to confess in a public forum. Remember that everyone is a sinner (Romans 3.23). We all need to confess and there is no better place to do that than in worship.

- **Corporate prayer must provide an opportunity for each believer to receive forgiveness.** The Bible makes it clear that everyone who repents of their sins will be forgiven (1 John 1.9). It is a truth that God will forgive those who repent. But I have a conviction that many humans, some of whom sit in church with you each week, have a hard time accepting that forgiveness, or of forgiving themselves. This may take time, prayer and counsel, but once God's grace is activated in our lives, it is done. We are forgiven.
- **Corporate prayer requires us to minister to the sick.** If there are members of your church who are ill and unable to attend worship, be sure to pray for them. Be certain to pray for those who are present, that they may be healed. I believe that the best way to pray for the sick is to use James 5 as a model. The instructions from that passage include:
  - Calling the elders of the church (James 5.13). Leaders of the congregation and other mature believers should be the ones leading in prayer for healing.
  - Anointing with oil. Oil is seen throughout the Bible as a symbol of the presence of the Holy Spirit. There are no requirements about the type or amount of oil to be used, but this step is a crucial mark of obedience.
  - Using the name of the Lord. Never forget that when we pray, no matter the purpose or

occasion, we are to pray according to God's will and in the name of Jesus.

- **Corporate prayer unites our hearts in petition before God.** This can be a question of style. In your church everyone can pray aloud at the same time, or one person can pray aloud with the rest of the congregation agreeing in silent prayer, or everyone in the church can pray silently at the same time. Any of these is acceptable (or, you may find that some other method works for you). But the end result of corporate prayer is that we have a singleness of heart and the congregation becomes one in Christ.

Church Basics 9: Elements of Worship
Sacraments and Holy Times

I am a United Methodist pastor and as such, I approach the sacraments from a decidedly United Methodist perspective. For the sake of this article, however, you should know that our worship services need to not only have times of sacramental experience, but should pursue and incorporate other holy times. I will speak from the perspective of Methodism, but I do not want this discussion to be partisan or exclusive in any way. Therefore, what follows should be appropriate for any congregation of any theological persuasion.

When we are talking about sacraments in general we refer to them as "an outward sign of an inward grace." This means simply that there are some sort of physical representations of the presence of Christ. In Holy Communion this is the bread and the juice that we use, and in baptism we think of the water in this way. These material manifestations demonstrate what is happening in the heart of the believer. It is not the water, or the bread, or the juice that are causing the work of God. God works in the heart of the believer of his own volition. These outward signs show what God is doing for us and for others as evidence of God's grace.

United Methodists practice the sacraments of baptism and communion. Other faith communities consider marriage, foot washing and confirmation, among others to also be sacraments. Again, I do not want to press my tradition onto another. Suffice it to say that whatever the tradition you find yourself in, you should allow, encourage and plan for dramatic experiences of God's presence in your worship times.

There are other times when we have encounters with the presence of God. What we have talked about so far could be characterized by saying that there are things that we do to invite the presence of God. There are also manifestations of the Holy Spirit that are other-worldly in origin. You have no doubt had a personal experience in which the presence of God brought you to tears, or caused you to shout. These "holy times" should also be encouraged.

- **Gifts of the Holy Spirit.** Although many abuses have taken place and extremism is definitely possible, remember that many of the gifts of the Holy Spirit consist of physical manifestations that should be allowed and encountered in the worshiping community and in private prayer times. Be cautious to not become legalistic about these gifts, but look for opportunities to experience the fullness of God through them.
- **The Presence of Glory.** There are times in worship when we can see the presence of the glory of God. We might experience a glow, a fog or a light of some sort that will indicate that God is present. My experiences have included times when I was unable to stand in worship because the glory of the Lord kept me in my seat.
- **Revelations and the voice of God.** First, a disclaimer: I have never heard the voice of God with my ears. But I often hear him speaking to me in my heart. He reveals his will to me and speaks to me about my life, my faith and my ministry. There are few things that are more moving or dramatic in a worship setting than hearing, without question, what God is saying.

Church Basics 10: Elements of Worship
A Welcoming Atmosphere

...love the stranger, for you were strangers in the land of Egypt. **Deuteronomy 10.19**

In worship the first impression you make is the most significant. Therefore, it is imperative that we focus on creating a loving and welcoming atmosphere for those around us. This should include, but definitely not be limited to men and women who are not like us. We need to be opening ourselves and our church to all sorts of people. Jesus has established the example for us. We are to love all people. Neighbors are welcome, as are foreigners. Include strangers and sinners. Treat everyone in the congregation, whether visitor or member, with respect, understanding and love.

Often Christian people pay lip service to this sort of thing. That is, we like to talk about loving all people. We tell the visitor that he is loved, but we don't often demonstrate love. In fact, it is often easier for people to legalistically judge the sins and shortcomings of those who are in need of God's grace. Don't do that. Tell people that you love them, and then show them that you do. Many churches in the west offer gifts to worship visitors as a sign of their love. Others sometimes offer special classes or programs as a demonstration of that love. It would be good for you to concern yourself and your church with the financial, spiritual, relational and physical needs of those in your church. Welcome newcomers by learning about their needs and helping them take steps to meet them.

One very practical way to show respect for new people- and all people- in worship is to use the language of the local community. Obviously this means that we use vocabulary that is familiar to the congregation, but it goes way beyond that. We should set our priorities and our programs according to the community in which we serve. Additionally, consider the culture in which your church exists before establishing worship times and locations. Church buildings should be appropriate for the city, village or rural area in which they exist. The wardrobe, jewelry and behavior of church leadership also needs to be consistent with the culture.

None of this should be used to suggest that the church should compromise the gospel or the practices of the faith. But we need to discern God's will in every situation. Never change anything that is specifically spelled out in the Bible. Be sensitive to non-essentials that can allow you to effectively reach your community.

By the way, this sensitivity may be the best way to show your concern, not only for people who visit your congregation, but to the whole community.

Use worship forms with which your people are comfortable. For example, in a new setting, a mission congregation, for example, a pastor in a clergy robe will likely cause more questions and difficulties than anything else. Consider the local community when deciding things like Bible translation, music style and procedures for prayer.

The bottom line for any church- new or existing- is to eliminate as many obstacles as possible. Always consider how your decisions will affect the atmosphere of your church. If it will discourage anyone from attending, hearing the gospel, or turning to Christ, be very cautious about pursuing it.

Appendix

Appendix Contents

- Appendix Contents
- Bible reading schedules/ plans
  - Year One- New Testament
  - Year Two- New Testament, Psalms, Proverbs
  - Year Three- Complete Bible
- Bible Memorization helps
- Bible memorization verses
- 630 Challenge
- Prayer Patterns
  - Psalm 103
  - ACTS
  - PATH
  - The Lord's Prayer
  - Praying the Scriptures
- Prayer Triplets
- Verses to Pray
- Romans Road Evangelism Plan
- John 3.16 Evangelism Plan
- ABC Bible Study
- Why Study the Bible?
- How to Study the Bible- Psalm 119
- Journaling Guidelines
- 4 I's Visit
- Starting a Faith Team
- Elements of a Faith Team/ Church
- Accountability and Discipleship Questions
- Faith Team Agenda (Sample Meeting)

Bible Reading Schedule
Year One- New Testament

Jan 1	Matthew 1		Feb 16	Mark 1.1-22
Jan 2	Matt 2		Feb 17	Mark 1.23-45
Jan 3	Matt 3		Feb 18	Mark 2
Jan 4	Matt 4		Feb 19	Mark 3.1-21
Jan 5	Matt 5.1-26		Feb 20	Mark 3.22-35
Jan 6	Matt 5.27-48		Feb 21	Mark 4.1-20
Jan 7	Matt 6		Feb 22	Mark 4.21-41
Jan 8	Matt 7		Feb 23	Mark 5.1-20
Jan 9	Matt 8		Feb 24	Mark 5.21-43
Jan 10	Matt 9.1-17		Feb 25	Mark 6.1-32
Jan 11	Matt 9.18-38		Feb 26	Mark 6.33-56
Jan 12	Matt 10.1-23		Feb 27	Mark 7.1-13
Jan 13	Matt 10.24-42		Feb 28	Mark 7.14-37
Jan 14	Matt 11		Mar 1	Mark 8.1-21
Jan 15	Matt 12.1-21		Mar 2	Mark 8.22-38
Jan 16	Matt 12.22-50		Mar 3	Mark 9.1-29
Jan 17	Matt 13.1-32		Mar 4	Mark 9.30-50
Jan 18	Matt 13.33-58		Mar 5	Mark 10.1-31
Jan 19	Matt 14.1-21		Mar 6	Mark 10.32-52
Jan 20	Matt 14.22-36		Mar 7	Mark 11.1-19
Jan 21	Matt 15.1-20		Mar 8	Mark 11.20-33
Jan 22	Matt 15.21-39		Mar 9	Mark 12.1-27
Jan 23	Matt 16		Mar 10	Mark 12.28-44
Jan 24	Matt 17		Mar 11	Mark 13.1-13
Jan 25	Matt 18.1-20		Mar 12	Mark 13.14-37
Jan 26	Matt 18.21-35		Mar 13	Mark 14.1-25
Jan 27	Matt 19.1-15		Mar 14	Mark 14.26-50
Jan 28	Matt 19.16-30		Mar 15	Mark 14.51-72
Jan 29	Matt 20. 1-16		Mar 16	Mark 15.1-26
Jan 30	Matt 20.17-34		Mar 17	Mark 15.27-47
Jan 31	Matt 21.1-22		Mar 18	Mark 16
Feb 1	Matt 21.23-46		Mar 19	Luke 1.1-23
Feb 2	Matt 22.1-22		Mar 20	Luke 1.24-56
Feb 3	Matt 22.23-46		Mar 21	Luke 1.57-80
Feb 4	Matt 23.1-22		Mar 22	Luke 2.1-24
Feb 5	Matt 23.23-39		Mar 23	Luke 2.25-52
Feb 6	Matt 24.1-22		Mar 24	Luke 3
Feb 7	Matt 24.23-51		Mar 25	Luke 4.1-32
Feb 8	Matt 25.1-30		Mar 26	Luke 4.33-44
Feb 9	Matt 25.31-46		Mar 27	Luke 5.1-16
Feb 10	Matt 26.1-19		Mar 28	Luke 5.17-39
Feb 11	Matt 26.20-54		Mar 29	Luke 6.1-26
Feb 12	Matt 26.55-75		Mar 30	Luke 6.27-49
Feb 13	Matt 27.1-31		Mar 31	Luke 7.1-30
Feb 14	Matt 27.32-66		Apr 1	Luke 7.31-50
Feb 15	Matt 28		Apr 2	Luke 8.1-21

Apr 3	Luke 8.22-56	May 24	John 9.1-23
Apr 4	Luke 9.1-36	May 25	John 9.24-41
Apr 5	Luke 9.37-64	May 26	John 10.1-21
Apr 6	Luke 10.1-24	May 27	John 10.22-42
Apr 7	Luke 10.25-42	May 28	John 11.1-17
Apr 8	Luke 11.1-28	May 29	John 11.18-46
Apr 9	Luke 11.29-54	May 30	John 11.47-57
Apr10	Luke 12.1-34	May 31	John 12.1-19
Apr 11	Luke 12.35-59	June 1	John 12.20-50
Apr 12	Luke 13	June 2	John 13.1-17
Apr 13	Luke 14.1-24	June 3	John 13.18-38
Apr 14	Luke 14.25-35	June 4	John 14
Apr 15	Luke 15.1-10	June 5	John 15
Apr 16	Luke 15.11-32	June 6	John 16.1-15
Apr 17	Luke 16.1-18	June 7	John 16.16-33
Apr 18	Luke 16.19-31	June 8	John 17
Apr 19	Luke 17.1-19	June 9	John 18.1-23
Apr 20	Luke 17.20-37	June 10	John 18.24-40
Apr 21	Luke 18.1-17	June 11	John 19.1-22
Apr 22	Luke 18.18-43	June 12	John 19.23-42
Apr 23	Luke 19.1-28	June 13	John 20
Apr 24	Luke 19.29-48	June 14	John 21
Apr 25	Luke 20.1-26	June 15	Acts 1
Apr 26	Luke 20.27-47	June 16	Acts 2.1-13
Apr 27	Luke 21.1-19	June 17	Acts 2.14-47
Apr 28	Luke 21.20-38	June 18	Acts 3
Apr 29	Luke 22.1-30	June 19	Acts 4.1-22
Apr 30	Luke 22.31-53	June 20	Acts 4.23-37
May 1	Luke 22.54-71	June 21	Acts 5.1-16
May 2	Luke 23.1-26	June 22	Acts 5.17-42
May 3	Luke 23.27-38	June 23	Acts 6
May 4	Luke 23.39-56	June 24	Acts 7.1-19
May 5	Luke 24.1-35	June 25	Acts 7.20-43
May 6	Luke 24.36-53	June 26	Acts 7.44-60
May 7	John 1.1-28	June 27	Acts 8.1-25
May 8	John 1.29-51	June 28	Acts 8.56-40
May 9	John 2	June 29	Acts 9.1-22
May 10	John 3.1-21	June 30	Acts 9.23-43
May 11	John 3.22-36	July 1	Acts 10.1-23
May 12	John 4.1-30	July 2	Acts 10.24-48
May 13	John 4.31-54	July 3	Acts 11
May 14	John 5.1-24	July 4	Acts 12
May 15	John 5.25-47	July 5	Acts 13.1-23
May 16	John 6.1-21	July 6	Acts 13.24-52
May 17	John 6.22-44	July 7	Acts 14
May 18	John 6.45-71	July 8	Acts 15.1-21
May 19	John 7.1-31	July 9	Acts 15.22-41
May 20	John 7.32-53	July 10	Acts 16.1-15
May 21	John 8.1-20	July 11	Acts 16.16-40
May 22	John 8.21-36	July 12	Acts 17.1-15
May 23	John 8.37-59	July 13	Acts 17.16-34

July 14	Acts 18	Sept 3	1 Cor 13
July 15	Acts 19.1-20	Sept 4	1 Cor 14.1-20
July 16	Acts 19.21-41	Sept 5	1 Cor 14.21-40
July 17	Acts 20.1-16	Sept 6	1 Cor 15.1-32
July 18	Acts 20.17-38	Sept 7	1 Cor 15.33-58
July 19	Acts 21.1-14	Sept 8	1 Cor 16
July 20	Acts 21.15-40	Sept 9	2 Corinthians 1
July 21	Acts 22	Sept 10	2 Cor 2
July 22	Acts 23.1-11	Sept 11	2 Cor 3
July 23	Acts 23.12-35	Sept 12	2 Cor 4
July 24	Acts 24	Sept 13	2 Cor 5
July 25	Acts 25	Sept 14	2 Cor 6
July 26	Acts 26	Sept 15	2 Cor 7
July 27	Acts 27.1-25	Sept 16	2 Cor 8
July 28	Acts 27.26-44	Sept 17	2 Cor 9
July 29	Acts 28.1-15	Sept 18	2 Cor 10
July 30	Acts 28.16-31	Sept 19	2 Cor 11.1-15
July 31	Romans 1	Sept 20	2 Cor 11.16-33
Aug 1	Romans 2	Sept 21	2 Cor 12
Aug 2	Romans 3	Sept 22	2 Cor 13
Aug 3	Romans 4	Sept 23	Galatians 1
Aug 4	Romans 5	Sept 24	Gal 2
Aug 5	Romans 6	Sept 25	Gal 3
Aug 6	Romans 7	Sept 26	Gal 4
Aug 7	Romans 8.1-18	Sept 27	Gal 5
Aug 8	Romans 8.19-39	Sept 28	Gal 6
Aug 9	Romans 9	Sept 29	Ephesians 1
Aug 10	Romans 10	Sept 30	Eph 2
Aug 11	Romans 11.1-21	Oct 1	Eph 3
Aug 12	Romans 11.22-36	Oct 2	Eph 4
Aug 13	Romans 12	Oct 3	Eph 5
Aug 14	Romans 13	Oct 4	Eph 6
Aug 15	Romans 14	Oct 5	Philippians 1
Aug 16	Romans 15.1-20	Oct 6	Phi 2
Aug 17	Romans 15.21-33	Oct 7	Phi 3
Aug 18	Romans 16	Oct 8	Phi 4
Aug 19	1 Corinthians 1	Oct 9	Colossians 1
Aug 20	1 Cor 2	Oct 10	Col 2
Aug 21	1 Cor 3	Oct 11	Col 3
Aug 22	1 Cor 4	Oct 12	Col 4
Aug 23	1 Cor 5	Oct 13	1 Thessalonians 1
Aug 24	1 Cor 6	Oct 14	1 Thes 2
Aug 25	1 Cor 7.1-24	Oct 15	1 Thes 3
Aug 26	1 Cor 7.25-40	Oct 16	1 Thes 4
Aug 27	1 Cor 8	Oct 17	1 Thes 5
Aug 28	1 Cor 9	Oct 18	2 Thessalonians 1
Aug 29	1 Cor 10.1-13	Oct 19	2 Thes 2
Aug 30	1 Cor 10.14-33	Oct 20	2 Thes 3
Aug 31	1 Cor 11.1-15	Oct 21	1 Timothy 1
Sept 1	1 Cor 11.16-34	Oct 22	1 Tim 2
Sept 2	1 Cor 12	Oct 23	1 Tim 3

Oct 24	1 Tim 4	Nov 28	1 Pet 5
Oct 25	1 Tim 5	Nov 29	2 Peter 1
Oct 26	1 Tim 6	Nov 30	2 Pet 2
Oct 27	2 Tim 1	Dec 1	2 Pet 3
Oct 28	2 Tim 2	Dec 2	1 John 1
Oct 29	2 Tim 3	Dec 3	1 John 2
Oct 30	2 Tim 4	Dec 4	1 John 3
Oct 31	Titus 1	Dec 5	1 John 4
Nov 1	Titus 2	Dec 6	1 John 5
Nov 2	Titus 3	Dec 7	2 John
Nov 3	Philemon	Dec 8	3 John
Nov 4	Hebrews 1	Dec 9	Jude
Nov 5	Heb 2	Dec 10	Revelation 1
Nov 6	Heb 3	Dec 11	Rev 2
Nov 7	Heb 4	Dec 12	Rev 3
Nov 8	Heb 5	Dec 13	Rev 4
Nov 9	Heb 6	Dec 14	Rev 5
Nov 10	Heb 7	Dec 15	Rev 6
Nov 11	Heb 8	Dec 16	Rev 7
Nov 12	Heb 9	Dec 17	Rev 8
Nov 13	Heb 10.1-23	Dec 18	Rev 9
Nov 14	Heb 10.24-39	Dec 19	Rev 10
Nov 15	Heb 11.1-19	Dec 20	Rev 11
Nov 16	Heb 11.20-40	Dec 21	Rev 12
Nov 17	Heb 12	Dec 22	Rev 13
Nov 18	Heb 13	Dec 23	Rev 14
Nov 19	James 1	Dec 24	Rev 15
Nov 20	Jas 2	Dec 25	Rev 16
Nov 21	Jas 3	Dec 26	Rev 17
Nov 22	Jas 4	Dec 27	Rev 18
Nov 23	Jas 5	Dec 28	Rev 19
Nov 24	1 Peter 1	Dec 29	Rev 20
Nov 25	1 Pet 2	Dec 30	Rev 21
Nov 26	1 Pet 3	Dec 31	Rev 22
Nov 27	1 Pet 4		

Bible Reading Schedule
Year Two- New Testament, Psalms, Proverbs

Jan 1	Matthew 1	Feb 16	Psalm 36-37	Apr 3	Luke 3
Jan 2	Matt 2	Feb 17	Psalm 38-39	Apr 4	Luke 4
Jan 3	Matt 3	Feb 18	Psalm 40-41	Apr 5	Luke 5
Jan 4	Matt 4	Feb 19	Psalm 42-43	Apr 6	Luke 6
Jan 5	Matt 5	Feb 20	Psalm 44-45	Apr 7	Luke 7
Jan 6	Matt 6	Feb 21	Psalm 46-47	Apr 8	Luke 8
Jan 7	Matt 7	Feb 22	Psalm 48-49	Apr 9	Luke 9
Jan 8	Matt 8	Feb 23	Psalm 50	Apr10	Luke 10
Jan 9	Matt 9	Feb 24	Psalm 51	Apr 11	Luke 11
Jan 10	Matt 10	Feb 25	Mark 1	Apr 12	Luke 12
Jan 11	Matt 11	Feb 26	Mark 2	Apr 13	Luke 13
Jan 12	Matt 12	Feb 27	Mark 3	Apr 14	Luke 14
Jan 13	Matt 13	Feb 28	Mark 4	Apr 15	Luke 15
Jan 14	Matt 14	Mar 1	Mark 5	Apr 16	Luke 16
Jan 15	Matt 15	Mar 2	Mark 6	Apr 17	Luke 17
Jan 16	Matt 16	Mar 3	Mark 7	Apr 18	Luke 18
Jan 17	Matt 17	Mar 4	Mark 8	Apr 19	Luke 19
Jan 18	Matt 18	Mar 5	Mark 9	Apr 20	Luke 20
Jan 19	Matt 19	Mar 6	Mark 10	Apr 21	Luke 21
Jan 20	Matt 20	Mar 7	Mark 11	Apr 22	Luke 22
Jan 21	Matt 21	Mar 8	Mark 12	Apr 23	Luke 23
Jan 22	Matt 22	Mar 9	Mark 13	Apr 24	Luke 24
Jan 23	Matt 23	Mar 10	Mark 14	Apr 25	Psalm 90-91
Jan 24	Matt 24	Mar 11	Mark 15	Apr 26	Psalm 92-93
Jan 25	Matt 25	Mar 12	Mark 16	Apr 27	Psalm 94-95
Jan 26	Matt 26	Mar 13	Psalm 52-54	Apr 28	Psalm 96-97
Jan 27	Matt 27	Mar 14	Psalm 55-56	Apr 29	Psalm 98-100
Jan 28	Matt 28	Mar 15	Psalm 57-59	Apr 30	Psalm 101-102
Jan 29	Psalm 1-2	Mar 16	Psalm 60-62	May 1	Psalm 103-104
Jan 30	Psalm 3-4	Mar 17	Psalm 63-64	May 2	Psalm 105
Jan 31	Psalm5-6	Mar 18	Psalm 65-66	May 3	Psalm 106
Feb 1	Psalm 7	Mar 19	Psalm 67-68	May 4	Psalm 107
Feb 2	Psalm 8-9	Mar 20	Psalm 69	May 5	Psalm 108-109
Feb 3	Psalm 10-11	Mar 21	Psalm 70-71	May 6	John 1
Feb 4	Psalm 12-13	Mar 22	Psalm 72	May 7	John 2
Feb 5	Psalm 14-15	Mar 23	Psalm 73	May 8	John 3
Feb 6	Psalm 16-17	Mar 24	Psalm 74	May 9	John 4
Feb 7	Psalm 18	Mar 25	Psalm 75-77	May 10	John 5
Feb 8	Psalm 19-20	Mar 26	Psalm 78	May 11	John 6
Feb 9	Psalm 21-22	Mar 27	Psalm 79-80	May 12	John 7
Feb 10	Psalm 23-24	Mar 28	Psalm 81-83	May 13	John 8
Feb 11	Psalm 25-26	Mar 29	Psalm 84-86	May 14	John 9
Feb 12	Psalm 27-29	Mar 30	Psalm 87-88	May 15	John 10
Feb 13	Psalm 30-31	Mar 31	Psalm 89	May 16	John 11
Feb 14	Psalm 32-33	Apr 1	Luke 1	May 17	John 12
Feb 15	Psalm 34-35	Apr 2	Luke 2	May 18	John 13

May 19	John 14	July 9	Psalm 143	Aug 29	1 Cor 12		
May 20	John 15	July 10	Psalm 144-145	Aug 30	1 Cor 13		
May 21	John 16	July 11	Psalm 146-147	Aug 31	1 Cor 14		
May 22	John 17	July 12	Psalm 148-149	Sept 1	1 Cor 15		
May 23	John 18	July 13	Psalm 150	Sept 2	1 Cor 16		
May 24	John 19	July 14	Romans 1	Sept 3	2 Corinthians 1		
May 25	John 20	July 15	Rom 2	Sept 4	2 Cor 2		
May 26	John 21	July 16	Rom 3	Sept 5	2 Cor 3		
May 27	Psalm 110-112	July 17	Rom 4	Sept 6	2 Cor 4		
May 28	Psalm 113-115	July 18	Rom 5	Sept 7	2 Cor 5		
May 29	Psalm 116-117	July 19	Rom 6	Sept 8	2 Cor 6		
May 30	Psalm 118	July 20	Rom 7	Sept 9	2 Cor 7		
May 31	Psalm 119.1-88	July 21	Rom 8	Sept 10	2 Cor 8		
June 1	Psalm 119.89-176	July 22	Rom 9	Sept 11	2 Cor 9		
June 2	Psalm 120-122	July 23	Rom 10	Sept 12	2 Cor 10		
June 3	Psalm 123-125	July 24	Rom 11	Sept 13	2 Cor 11		
June 4	Psalm 126-128	July 25	Rom 12	Sept 14	2 Cor 12		
June 5	Psalm 129-131	July 26	Rom 13	Sept 15	2 Cor 13		
June 6	Psalm 132-134	July 27	Rom 14	Sept 16	Proverbs 20		
June 7	Acts 1	July 28	Rom 15	Sept 17	Prov 21		
June 8	Acts 2	July 29	Rom 16	Sept 18	Prov 22		
June 9	Acts 3	July 30	Proverbs 1	Sept 19	Prov 23		
June 10	Acts 4	July 31	Prov 2	Sept 20	Prov 24		
June 11	Acts 5	Aug 1	Prov 3	Sept 21	Prov 25		
June 12	Acts 6	Aug 2	Prov 4	Sept 22	Prov 26		
June 13	Acts 7	Aug 3	Prov 5	Sept 23	Prov 27		
June 14	Acts 8	Aug 4	Prov 6	Sept 24	Prov 28		
June 15	Acts 9	Aug 5	Prov 7	Sept 25	Prov 29		
June 16	Acts 10	Aug 6	Prov 8	Sept 26	Prov 30		
June 17	Acts 11	Aug 7	Prov 9	Sept 27	Prov 31		
June 18	Acts 12	Aug 8	Prov 10	Sept 28	Galatians 1		
June 19	Acts 13	Aug 9	Prov 11	Sept 29	Gal 2		
June 20	Acts 14	Aug 10	Prov 12	Sept 30	Gal 3		
June 21	Acts 15	Aug 11	Prov 13	Oct 1	Gal 4		
June 22	Acts 16	Aug 12	Prov 14	Oct 2	Gal 5		
June 23	Acts 17	Aug 13	Prov 15	Oct 3	Gal 6		
June 24	Acts 18	Aug 14	Prov 16	Oct 4	Ephesians 1		
June 25	Acts 19	Aug 15	Prov 17	Oct 5	Eph 2		
June 26	Acts 20	Aug 16	Prov 18	Oct 6	Eph 3		
June 27	Acts 21	Aug 17	Prov 19	Oct 7	Eph 4		
June 28	Acts 22	Aug 18	1 Corinthians 1	Oct 8	Eph 5		
June 29	Acts 23	Aug 19	1 Cor 2	Oct 9	Eph 6		
June 30	Acts 24	Aug 20	1 Cor 3	Oct 10	Philippians 1		
July 1	Acts 25	Aug 21	1 Cor 4	Oct 11	Phil 2		
July 2	Acts 26	Aug 22	1 Cor 5	Oct 12	Phil 3		
July 3	Acts 27	Aug 23	1 Cor 6	Oct 13	Phil 4		
July 4	Acts 28	Aug 24	1 Cor 7	Oct 14	Colossians 1		
July 5	Psalm 135-136	Aug 25	1 Cor 8	Oct 15	Col 2		
July 6	Psalm 137-138	Aug 26	1 Cor 9	Oct 16	Col 3		
July 7	Psalm 139-140	Aug 27	1 Cor 10	Oct 17	Col 4		
July 8	Psalm 141-142	Aug 28	1 Cor 11	Oct 18	1 Thessalonians 1		

● ● ●

Oct 19	1 Thes 2	Nov 13	Heb 5	Dec 8	2 & 3 John
Oct 20	1 Thes 3	Nov 14	Heb 6	Dec 9	Jude
Oct 21	1 Thes 4	Nov 15	Heb 7	Dec 10	Revelation 1
Oct 22	1 Thes 5	Nov 16	Heb 8	Dec 11	Rev 2
Oct 23	2 Thes 1	Nov 17	Heb 9	Dec 12	Rev 3
Oct 24	2 Thes 2	Nov 18	Heb 10	Dec 13	Rev 4
Oct 25	2 Thes 3	Nov 19	Heb 11	Dec 14	Rev 5
Oct 26	1 Timothy 1	Nov 20	Heb 12	Dec 15	Rev 6
Oct 27	1 Tim 2	Nov 21	Heb 13	Dec 16	Rev 7
Oct 28	1 Tim 3	Nov 22	James 1	Dec 17	Rev 8
Oct 29	1 Tim 4	Nov 23	Jas 2	Dec 18	Rev 9
Oct 30	1 Tim 5	Nov 24	Jas 3	Dec 19	Rev 10
Oct 31	1 Tim 6	Nov 25	Jas 4	Dec 20	Rev 11
Nov 1	2 Tim 1	Nov 26	Jas 5	Dec 21	Rev 12
Nov 2	2 Tim 2	Nov 27	1 Peter 1	Dec 22	Rev 13
Nov 3	2 Tim 3	Nov 28	1 Pet 2	Dec 23	Rev 14
Nov 4	2 Tim 4	Nov 29	1 Pet 3	Dec 24	Rev 15
Nov 5	Titus 1	Nov 30	1 Pet 4-5	Dec 25	Rev 16
Nov 6	Titus 2	Dec 1	2 Pet 1	Dec 26	Rev 17
Nov 7	Titus 3	Dec 2	2 Pet 2	Dec 27	Rev 18
Nov 8	Philemon	Dec 3	2 Pet 3	Dec 28	Rev 19
Nov 9	Hebrews 1	Dec 4	1 John 1-2	Dec 29	Rev 20
Nov 10	Heb 2	Dec 5	1 John 3	Dec 30	Rev 21
Nov 11	Heb 3	Dec 6	1 John 4	Dec 31	Rev 22
Nov 12	Heb 4	Dec 7	1 John 5		

Bible Schedule
Year Three- Complete Bible

Jan 1	Matthew 1	Genesis 1-2	Feb 17	Mark 1.23-45	Lev 24-25
Jan 2	Matt 2	Gen 3-5	Feb 18	Mark 2	Lev 26-27
Jan 3	Matt 3	Gen 6-8	Feb 19	Mark 3.1-21	Numbers 1-2
Jan 4	Matt 4	Gen 9-11	Feb 20	Mark 3.22-35	Num 3-4
Jan 5	Matt 5.1-26	Gen 12-14	Feb 21	Mark 4.1-20	Num 5-6
Jan 6	Matt 5.27-48	Gen 15-17	Feb 22	Mark 4.21-41	Num 7-8
Jan 7	Matt 6	Gen 18-19	Feb 23	Mark 5.1-20	Num 9-11
Jan 8	Matt 7	Gen 20-22	Feb 24	Mark 5.21-43	Num 12-14
Jan 9	Matt 8	Gen 23-24	Feb 25	Mark 6.1-32	Num 15-17
Jan 10	Matt 9.1-17	Gen 25-26	Feb 26	Mark 6.33-56	Num 18-20
Jan 11	Matt 9.18-38	Gen 27-28	Feb 27	Mark 7.1-13	Num 21-22
Jan 12	Matt 10.1-23	Gen 29-30	Feb 28	Mark 7.14-37	Num 23-25
Jan 13	Matt 10.24-42	Gen 31-32	Mar 1	Mark 8.1-21	Num 26-27
Jan 14	Matt 11	Gen 33-35	Mar 2	Mark 8.22-38	Num 28-29
Jan 15	Matt 12.1-21	Gen 36-37	Mar 3	Mark 9.1-29	Num 30-31
Jan 16	Matt 12.22-50	Gen 38-40	Mar 4	Mark 9.30-50	Num 32-33
Jan 17	Matt 13.1-32	Gen 41	Mar 5	Mark 10.1-31	Num 34-36
Jan 18	Matt 13.33-58	Gen 42-43	Mar 6	Mark 10.32-52	Deut 1-2
Jan 19	Matt 14.1-21	Gen 44-45	Mar 7	Mark 11.1-19	De 3-4
Jan 20	Matt 14.22-36	Gen 46-48	Mar 8	Mark 11.20-33	De 5-7
Jan 21	Matt 15.1-20	Gen 49-50	Mar 9	Mark 12.1-27	De 8-10
Jan 22	Matt 15.21-39	Exodus 1-3	Mar 10	Mark 12.28-44	De 11-13
Jan 23	Matt 16	Ex 4-6	Mar 11	Mark 13.1-13	De 14-16
Jan 24	Matt 17	Ex 7-8	Mar 12	Mark 13.14-37	De 17-19
Jan 25	Matt 18.1-20	Ex 9-10	Mar 13	Mark 14.1-25	De 20-22
Jan 26	Matt 18.21-35	Ex 11-12	Mar 14	Mark 14.26-50	De 23-25
Jan 27	Matt 19.1-15	Ex 13-15	Mar 15	Mark 14.51-72	De 26-27
Jan 28	Matt 19.16-30	Ex 16-18	Mar 16	Mark 15.1-26	De 28
Jan 29	Matt 20. 1-16	Ex 19-21	Mar 17	Mark 15.27-47	De 29-30
Jan 30	Matt 20.17-34	Ex 22-24	Mar 18	Mark 16	De 31-32
Jan 31	Matt 21.1-22	Ex 25-26	Mar 19	Luke 1.1-23	De 33-34
Feb 1	Matt 21.23-46	Ex 27-28	Mar 20	Luke 1.24-56	Joshua 1-3
Feb 2	Matt 22.1-22	Ex 29-30	Mar 21	Luke 1.57-80	Jos 4-6
Feb 3	Matt 22.23-46	Ex 31-33	Mar 22	Luke 2.1-24	Jos 7-8
Feb 4	Matt 23.1-22	Ex 34-36	Mar 23	Luke 2.25-52	Jos 9-10
Feb 5	Matt 23.23-39	Ex 37-38	Mar 24	Luke 3	Jos 11-13
Feb 6	Matt 24.1-22	Ex 39-40	Mar 25	Luke 4.1-32	Jos 14-15
Feb 7	Matt 24.23-51	Leviticus 1-3	Mar 26	Luke 4.33-44	Jos 16-18
Feb 8	Matt 25.1-30	Lev 4-6	Mar 27	Luke 5.1-16	Jos 19-20
Feb 9	Matt 25.31-46	Lev 7-9	Mar 28	Luke 5.17-39	Jos 21-22
Feb 10	Matt 26.1-19	Lev 10-12	Mar 29	Luke 6.1-26	Jos 23-24
Feb 11	Matt 26.20-54	Lev 13	Mar 30	Luke 6.27-49	Judges 1-2
Feb 12	Matt 26.55-75	Lev 14	Mar 31	Luke 7.1-30	Ju 3-5
Feb 13	Matt 27.1-31	Lev 15-17	Apr 1	Luke 7.31-50	Ju 6-7
Feb 14	Matt 27.32-66	Lev 18-19	Apr 2	Luke 8.1-21	Ju 8-9
Feb 15	Matt 28	Lev 20-21	Apr 3	Luke 8.22-56	Ju 10-11
Feb 16	Mark 1.1-22	Lev 22-23	Apr 4	Luke 9.1-36	Ju 12-14

Apr 5	Luke 9.37-64	Ju -15-17	May 26	John 10.1-21	1 Chr 17-19
Apr 6	Luke 10.1-24	Ju 18-19	May 27	John 10.22-42	1 Chr 20-22
Apr 7	Luke 10.25-42	Ju 20-21	May 28	John 11.1-17	1 Chr 23-25
Apr 8	Luke 11.1-28	Ruth	May 29	John 11.18-46	1 Chr 26-27
Apr 9	Luke 11.29-54	1 Samuel 1-3	May 30	John 11.47-57	1 Chr 28-29
Apr10	Luke 12.1-34	1 Sam 4-6	May 31	John 12.1-19	2 Chron 1-3
Apr 11	Luke 12.35-59	1 Sam 7-9	June 1	John 12.20-50	2 Chr 4-6
Apr 12	Luke 13	1 Sam 10-12	June 2	John 13.1-17	2 Chr 7-9
Apr 13	Luke 14.1-24	1 Sam 13-14	June 3	John 13.18-38	2 Chr 10-12
Apr 14	Luke 14.25-35	1 Sam 15-16	June 4	John 14	2 Chr 13-16
Apr 15	Luke 15.1-10	1 Sam 17-18	June 5	John 15	2 Chr 17-19
Apr 16	Luke 15.11-32	1 Sam 19-21	June 6	John 16.1-15	2 Chr 20-22
Apr 17	Luke 16.1-18	1 Sam 22-24	June 7	John 16.16-33	2 Chr 23-25
Apr 18	Luke 16.19-31	1 Sam 25-26	June 8	John 17	2 Chr 26-28
Apr 19	Luke 17.1-19	1 Sam 27-29	June 9	John 18.1-23	2 Chr 29-31
Apr 20	Luke 17.20-37	1 Sam 30-31	June 10	John 18.24-40	2 Chr 32-33
Apr 21	Luke 18.1-17	2 Samuel 1-3	June 11	John 19.1-22	2 Chr 34-36
Apr 22	Luke 18.18-43	2 Sam 4-6	June 12	John 19.23-42	Ezra 1-2
Apr 23	Luke 19.1-28	2 Sam 7-9	June 13	John 20	Ezr 3-5
Apr 24	Luke 19.29-48	2 Sam 10-12	June 14	John 21	Ezr 6-8
Apr 25	Luke 20.1-26	2 Sam 13-14	June 15	Acts 1	Ezr 9-10
Apr 26	Luke 20.27-47	2 Sam 15-16	June 16	Acts 2.1-13	Neh 1-3
Apr 27	Luke 21.1-19	2 Sam 17-18	June 17	Acts 2.14-47	Neh 4-6
Apr 28	Luke 21.20-38	2 Sam 19-20	June 18	Acts 3	Neh 7-8
Apr 29	Luke 22.1-30	2 Sam 21-22	June 19	Acts 4.1-22	Neh 9-11
Apr 30	Luke 22.31-53	2 Sam 23-24	June 20	Acts 4.23-37	Neh 12-13
May 1	Luke 22.54-71	1 Kings 1-2	June 21	Acts 5.1-16	Esther 1-3
May 2	Luke 23.1-26	1 Kin 3-5	June 22	Acts 5.17-42	Est 4-6
May 3	Luke 23.27-38	1 Kin 6-7	June 23	Acts 6	Est 7-10
May 4	Luke 23.39-56	1 Kin 8-9	June 24	Acts 7.1-19	Job 1-3
May 5	Luke 24.1-35	1 Kin 10-11	June 25	Acts 7.20-43	Job 4-6
May 6	Luke 24.36-53	1 Kin 12-13	June 26	Acts 7.44-60	Job 7-9
May 7	John 1.1-28	1 Kin 14-15	June 27	Acts 8.1-25	Job 10-12
May 8	John 1.29-51	1 Kin 16-18	June 28	Acts 8.56-40	Job 13-15
May 9	John 2	1 Kin 19-20	June 29	Acts 9.1-22	Job 16-18
May 10	John 3.1-21	1 Kin 21-22	June 30	Acts 9.23-43	Job 19-20
May 11	John 3.22-36	2 Kings 1-3	July 1	Acts 10.1-23	Job 21-22
May 12	John 4.1-30	2 Kin 4-5	July 2	Acts 10.24-48	Job 23-25
May 13	John 4.31-54	2 Kin 6-8	July 3	Acts 11	Job 26-28
May 14	John 5.1-24	2 Kin 9-11	July 4	Acts 12	Job 29-30
May 15	John 5.25-47	2 Kin 12-14	July 5	Acts 13.1-23	Job 31-32
May 16	John 6.1-21	2 Kin 15-17	July 6	Acts 13.24-52	Job 33-34
May 17	John 6.22-44	2 Kin 18-19	July 7	Acts 14	Job 35-37
May 18	John 6.45-71	2 Kin 20-22	July 8	Acts 15.1-21	Job 38-39
May 19	John 7.1-31	2 Kin 23-25	July 9	Acts 15.22-41	Job 40-42
May 20	John 7.32-53	1 Chron 1-2	July 10	Acts 16.1-15	Psalm 1-3
May 21	John 8.1-20	1 Chr 3-5	July 11	Acts 16.16-40	Psa 4-6
May 22	John 8.21-36	1 Chr 6-7	July 12	Acts 17.1-15	Psa 7-9
May 23	John 8.37-59	1 Chr 8-10	July 13	Acts 17.16-34	Psa 10-12
May 24	John 9.1-23	1 Chr 11-13	July 14	Acts 18	Psa 13-16
May 25	John 9.24-41	1 Chr 14-16	July 15	Acts 19.1-20	Psa 17-18

July 16	Acts 19.21-41	Psa 19-21	Sept 5	1 Cor 14.21-40	Pr 7-8
July 17	Acts 20.1-16	Psa 22-24	Sept 6	1 Cor 15.1-32	Pr 9-10
July 18	Acts 20.17-38	Psa 25-27	Sept 7	1 Cor 15.33-58	Pr 11-12
July 19	Acts 21.1-14	Psa 28-30	Sept 8	1 Cor 16	Pr 13-14
July 20	Acts 21.15-40	Psa 31-33	Sept 9	2 Corinthians 1	Pr 15-16
July 21	Acts 22	Psa 34-35	Sept 10	2 Cor 2	Pr 17-18
July 22	Acts 23.1-11	Psa 36-37	Sept 11	2 Cor 3	Pr 19-20
July 23	Acts 23.12-35	Psa 38-40	Sept 12	2 Cor 4	Pr 21-22
July 24	Acts 24	Psa 41-43	Sept 13	2 Cor 5	Pr 23-24
July 25	Acts 25	Psa 44-46	Sept 14	2 Cor 6	Pr 25-27
July 26	Acts 26	Psa 47-49	Sept 15	2 Cor 7	Pr 28-29
July 27	Acts 27.1-25	Psa 50-52	Sept 16	2 Cor 8	Pr 30-31
July 28	Acts 27.26-44	Psa 53-55	Sept 17	2 Cor 9	Eccles 1-3
July 29	Acts 28.1-15	Psa 56-58	Sept 18	2 Cor 10	Ecc 4-6
July 30	Acts 28.16-31	Psa 59-61	Sept 19	2 Cor 11.1-15	Ecc 7-9
July 31	Romans 1	Psa -2-64	Sept 20	2 Cor 11.16-33	Ecc 10-12
Aug 1	Romans 2	Psa 65-67	Sept 21	2 Cor 12	Song 1-3
Aug 2	Romans 3	Psa 68-69	Sept 22	2 Cor 13	Song 4-5
Aug 3	Romans 4	Psa 70-72	Sept 23	Galatians 1	Song 6-8
Aug 4	Romans 5	Psa 73-74	Sept 24	Gal 2	Isaiah 1-3
Aug 5	Romans 6	Psa 75-77	Sept 25	Gal 3	Is 4-6
Aug 6	Romans 7	Psa 78	Sept 26	Gal 4	Is 7-9
Aug 7	Romans 8.1-18	Psa 79-81	Sept 27	Gal 5	Is 10-12
Aug 8	Romans 8.19-39	Psa 82-84	Sept 28	Gal 6	Is 13-15
Aug 9	Romans 9	Psa 85-87	Sept 29	Ephesians 1	Is 16-18
Aug 10	Romans 10	Psa 88-89	Sept 30	Eph 2	Is 19-21
Aug 11	Romans 11.1-21	Psa 90-92	Oct 1	Eph 3	Is 22-23
Aug 12	Romans 11.22-36	Psa 93-95	Oct 2	Eph 4	Is 24-26
Aug 13	Romans 12	Psa 96-98	Oct 3	Eph 5	Is 27-28
Aug 14	Romans 13	Psa 99-102	Oct 4	Eph 6	Is 29-30
Aug 15	Romans 14	Psa 103-104	Oct 5	Philippians 1	Is 31-33
Aug 16	Romans 15.1-20	Psa 105-106	Oct 6	Phi 2	Is 34-36
Aug 17	Romans 15.21-33	Psa 107-108	Oct 7	Phi 3	Is 37-38
Aug 18	Romans 16	Psa 109-111	Oct 8	Phi 4	Is 39-40
Aug 19	1 Corinthians 1	Psa 112-115	Oct 9	Colossians 1	Is 41-42
Aug 20	1 Cor 2	Psa 116-118	Oct 10	Col 2	Is 43-44
Aug 21	1 Cor 3	Psa 119.1-48	Oct 11	Col 3	Is 45-47
Aug 22	1 Cor 4	Psa 119.49-104	Oct 12	Col 4	Is 48-49
Aug 23	1 Cor 5	Psa 119.105-176	Oct 13	1 Thessalonians 1	Is 50-52
Aug 24	1 Cor 6	Psa 120-123	Oct 14	1 Thes 2	Is 53-55
Aug 25	1 Cor 7.1-24	Psa 124-127	Oct 15	1 Thes 3	Is 56-58
Aug 26	1 Cor 7.25-40	Psa 128-131	Oct 16	1 Thes 4	Is 59-61
Aug 27	1 Cor 8	Psa 132-135	Oct 17	1 Thes 5	Is 62-64
Aug 28	1 Cor 9	Psa 136-138	Oct 18	2 Thessalonians 1	Is 65-66
Aug 29	1 Cor 10.1-13	Psa 139-141	Oct 19	2 Thes 2	Jeremiah 1-2
Aug 30	1 Cor 10.14-33	Psa 142-144	Oct 20	2 Thes 3	Jer 3-4
Aug 31	1 Cor 11.1-15	Psa 145-147	Oct 21	1 Timothy 1	Jer 5-6
Sept 1	1 Cor 11.16-34	Psa 148-150	Oct 22	1 Tim 2	Jer 7-8
Sept 2	1 Cor 12	Proverbs 1-2	Oct 23	1 Tim 3	Jer 9-10
Sept 3	1 Cor 13	Pr 3-4	Oct 24	1 Tim 4	Jer 11-13
Sept 4	1 Cor 14.1-20	Pr 5-6	Oct 25	1 Tim 5	Jer 14-16

Oct 26	1 Tim 6	Jer 17-19	Nov 29	2 Peter 1		Ez 41-42
Oct 27	2 Tim 1	Jer 20-22	Nov 30	2 Pet 2		Ez 43-44
Oct 28	2 Tim 2	Jer 23-24	Dec 1	2 Pet 3		Ez 45-46
Oct 29	2 Tim 3	Jer 25-26	Dec 2	1 John 1		Ez 47-48
Oct 30	2 Tim 4	Jer 27-28	Dec 3	1 John 2		Daniel 1-2
Oct 31	Titus 1	Jer 29-30	Dec 4	1 John 3		Dan 3-4
Nov 1	Titus 2	Jer 31-32	Dec 5	1 John 4		Dan 5-6
Nov 2	Titus 3	Jer 33-35	Dec 6	1 John 5		Dan 7-8
Nov 3	Philemon	Jer 36-37	Dec 7	2 John		Dan 9-10
Nov 4	Hebrews 1	Jer 38-39	Dec 8	3 John		Dan 11-12
Nov 5	Heb 2	Jer 40-42	Dec 9	Jude		Hosea 1-4
Nov 6	Heb 3	Jer 43-45	Dec 10	Revelation 1		Hos 5-8
Nov 7	Heb 4	Jer 46-48	Dec 11	Rev 2		Hos 9-11
Nov 8	Heb 5	Jer 49-50	Dec 12	Rev 3		Hos 12-14
Nov 9	Heb 6	Jer 51-52	Dec 13	Rev 4		Joel
Nov 10	Heb 7	Lament 1-2	Dec 14	Rev 5		Amos 1-3
Nov 11	Heb 8	Lam 3-5	Dec 15	Rev 6		Am 4-6
Nov 12	Heb 9	Ezekiel 1-3	Dec 16	Rev 7		Am 7-9
Nov 13	Heb 10.1-23	Ez 4-6	Dec 17	Rev 8		Obadiah
Nov 14	Heb 10.24-39	Ez 7-9	Dec 18	Rev 9		Jonah
Nov 15	Heb 11.1-19	Ez 10-12	Dec 19	Rev 10		Micah 1-3
Nov 16	Heb 11.20-40	Ez 13-15	Dec 20	Rev 11		Mic 4-5
Nov 17	Heb 12	Ez 16	Dec 21	Rev 12		Mic 6-7
Nov 18	Heb 13	Ez 17-19	Dec 22	Rev 13		Nahum
Nov 19	James 1	Ez 20-21	Dec 23	Rev 14		Habakkuk
Nov 20	Jas 2	Ez 22-23	Dec 24	Rev 15		Zephaniah
Nov 21	Jas 3	Ez 24-26	Dec 25	Rev 16		Haggai
Nov 22	Jas 4	Ez 27-28	Dec 26	Rev 17		Zechariah 1-3
Nov 23	Jas 5	Ez 29-31	Dec 27	Rev 18		Zec 4-6
Nov 24	1 Peter 1	Ez 32-33	Dec 28	Rev 19		Zec 7-9
Nov 25	1 Pet 2	Ez 34-35	Dec 29	Rev 20		Zec 10-12
Nov 26	1 Pet 3	Ez 36-37	Dec 30	Rev 21		Zec 13-14
Nov 27	1 Pet 4	Ez 38-39	Dec 31	Rev 22		Malachi
Nov 28	1 Pet 5	Ez 40				

Scripture Memory

There are several reasons that the follower of Jesus should make an effort to memorize the Bible and passages from it.

- We should memorize the Bible to follow the example that was set by Jesus himself. (Matthew 4.4, 7, 9)

- We should memorize the Bible to fill our minds with pure thoughts. (Psalm 119.9, 11)

- We should memorize the Bible so that we can be equipped for service to the Lord. (2 Timothy 3.16-17)

Memorization Methods-

Here are some ways that you can practice and use to memorize Bible verses.

- The Habitual Sequence Method. Repeat the topic of the verse, the verse reference, the content of the verse, and the reference again. Do this several times as you learn each verse.

- The Review Method. In this method you simply repeat the text over and over until you have committed it to memory. You can do this aloud or silently.

- The Transcription Method. Using an ordinary notebook, write the verse several times. You can even read it aloud or recite it as you are writing. The more frequently you do this the easier the memorization will become.

- The 'Aloud' Method. Read your passage aloud several times. Then repeat it aloud from memory.

- The Partner Method. With a partner (or small group) covenant to memorize verses together. The accountability and camaraderie will make the task easier.

Verses to Memorize

Jesus wept. **John 11.35**

For God so loved the world that He gave His only begotten Son, that whoever believes in Him should not perish but have everlasting life. **John 3.16**

Go therefore and make disciples of all the nations, baptizing them in the name of the Father and of the Son and of the Holy Spirit. **Matthew 28.19**

Jesus said to him, "I am the way, the truth, and the life. No one comes to the Father except through Me. **John 14.6**

For all have sinned and fall short of the glory of God. **Romans 3.23**

And we know that all things work together for good to those who love God, to those who are the called according to His purpose. **Romans 8.28**

I beseech you therefore, brethren, by the mercies of God, that you present your bodies a living sacrifice, holy, acceptable to God, which is your reasonable service. 2 And do not be conformed to this world, but be transformed by the renewing of your mind, that you may prove what is that good and acceptable and perfect will of God. **Romans 12.1-2**

For I know the thoughts that I think toward you, says

the Lord, thoughts of peace and not of evil, to give you a future and a hope. **Jeremiah 29.11**

A soft answer turns away wrath, But a harsh word stirs up anger. **Proverbs 15.1**

If we confess our sins, He is faithful and just to forgive us our sins and to cleanse us from all unrighteousness. 1 John 1.9

I can do all things through Christ who strengthens me. **Philippians 4.13**

Trust in the LORD with all your heart, And lean not on your own understanding; In all your ways acknowledge Him, And He shall direct your paths. **Proverbs 3.5-6**

There is none righteous, no, not one. **Romans 3.10**

For by grace you have been saved through faith, and that not of yourselves; it is the gift of God. **Ephesians 2.8**

And be kind to one another, tenderhearted, forgiving one another, even as God in Christ forgave you. **Ephesians 4.32**

Pray without ceasing, in everything give thanks; for this is the will of God in Christ Jesus for you. **1 Thessalonians 5.17-18**

But the Lord said to Samuel, "Do not look at his

appearance or at his physical stature, because I have refused him. For the LORD *does not see as man sees; for man looks at the outward appearance, but the Lord looks at the heart.* **1 Samuel 6.7**

For God has not given us a spirit of fear, but of power and of love and of a sound mind.
2 Timothy 1.7

Call to Me, and I will answer you, and show you great and mighty things, which you do not know. **Jeremiah 33.3**

And if it seems evil to you to serve the Lord, choose for yourselves this day whom you will serve, whether the gods which your fathers served that were on the other side of the River, or the gods of the Amorites, in whose land you dwell. But as for me and my house, we will serve the Lord."
Joshua 24.15

But seek first the kingdom of God and His righteousness, and all these things shall be added to you. **Matthew 6.33**

Judge not, that you be not judged. **Matthew 7.1**

Therefore, if anyone is in Christ, he is a new creation; old things have passed away; behold, all things have become new. **2 Corinthians 5.17**

But you shall receive power when the Holy Spirit has come upon you; and you shall be witnesses to Me in

*Jerusalem, and in all Judea and Samaria, and to the end of the earth." **Acts 1.8***

Let the word of Christ dwell in you richly in all wisdom, teaching and admonishing one another in psalms and hymns and spiritual songs, singing with grace in your hearts to the Lord.
Colossians 3.16

*Entreat me not to leave you, Or to turn back from following after you; For wherever you go, I will go; And wherever you lodge, I will lodge; Your people shall be my people, And your God, my God. Where you die, I will die, And there will I be buried. The LORD do so to me, and more also, If anything but death parts you and me." **Ruth 1.16-17***

The '630' Challenge

The '630' Challenge is another opportunity to read the Bible, but more importantly, to instill the content of the Bible into your head- and your heart. The challenge is to read the New Testament every month. To accomplish this feat, it will take reading about 10 chapters each day, six days each week for 30 days.

If you are able to complete the task for one year, you will have read the New Testament 12 times and will be more familiar with the word of God than ever. Knowing God's word in this way will change your life... forever!

Remember:
> 10 chapters a day
> six days a week
> one month

____	Day One	Matthew 1-10
____	Day Two	Matthew 11-20
____	Day Three	Matthew 11-Mark 2
____	Day Four	Mark 3-12
____	Day Five	Mark 13-Luke 5
____	Day Six	Luke 6-15
____	Day Seven	Luke 16-John 2
____	Day Eight	John 3-12
____	Day Nine	John 13-Acts 1
____	Day 10	Acts 2-11
____	Day 11	Acts 12-21
____	Day 12	Acts 22-Romans 3
____	Day 13	Romans 4-13
____	Day 14	Romans 14-1 Corinthians 7
____	Day 15	1 Corinthians 7-2 Corinthians 1
____	Day 16	2 Corinthians 2-11
____	Day 17	2 Corinthians 12- Ephesians 2
____	Day 18	Ephesians 3-Colossians 2
____	Day 19	Colossians 3- 2 Thessalonians 3
____	Day 20	1 Timothy 1- 2 Timothy 4
____	Day 21	Titus 1- Hebrews 6
____	Day 22	Hebrews 7- James 3
____	Day 23	James 4-2 Peter 3
____	Day 24	1 John 1- Revelation 2
____	Day 25	Revelation 3-12
____	Day 26	Revelation 13-22

Psalm 103 Prayer Model

Step 1. Praise the Lord. vv. 1-2
    Praise God for who he is and what he has done
    Thank him for his care and answering prayers

Step 2. Pray for blessings. v. 2
    Ask God to bless your church
    Pray blessings on your family, neighbors, friends
    Ask God to bless you

Step 3. Pray for pardon. v. 3
    Confess and repent of your sins
    Receive God's grace and pardon

Step 4. Pray for healing. v. 3
    Ask God for healing for yourself and others
    Pray for healing in your body, emotions,
    relationships, spirit

Step 5. Pray for redemption. v. 4
    Pray for those who are unsaved
    Ask God to renew the joy of your salvation

Step 6. Pray for loving kindness. v. 4
    Pray that you might be more loving to others
    Pray to receive the other fruits of the Holy Spirit

Step 7. Pray for renewal. v. 5
    Ask for your passion to be restored
    Request a renewed spirit from the Holy Spirit

The ACTS Model

Adoration- In this first part of your prayer time you should focus on worship and praising God. Use your imagination to exalt God in your life. Glorifying God is a challenge at first, but can quickly become the most rewarding part of your prayer time.

- Praise God for the creation.
- Praise God because he is the only one worthy of our praise.
- Offer to God the glory and honor reserved for him alone.
- Worship God because he desires our fellowship and worship.

Confession- This is the part of the prayer in which we confess our sins. Repentance is a key ingredient in this very important part of our prayer life.

- Confess sins of commission- that is, things that we do that we should not.
- Confess sins of omission- that is, things that we should do, but do not.

Thanksgiving- In this area of prayer we show God how thankful we are for all that he has done for us. Some items in this area will be very basic, others will be specific to our individual lives.

- Offer thanks to God for life, for sustenance and

for bounty.
- Offer thanks to God for the gift of salvation through faith in Christ.
- Offer thanks to God for blessings he has given you: Family, home, job, security, church, fellowship.
- Offer thanks for specific answers to prayer.

Supplication- This is the area in which we often confine our prayers. We should only give our requests to God after we have worshiped, confessed and thanked God, however. Requests can range from general to very specific.

- Pray for you Bishop, pastor and other church leaders.
- Pray for the mission and ministry of the church.
- Pray for our families, schools and governments.
- Pray for community leaders.
- Pray for the sick, handicapped and needy.
- Pray for the salvation of the lost.

The PATH Model

Praise- Begin your prayer time by listing the attributes of God and praising him for who he is.

- Praise God because he is omniscient. He knows all that there is to know.
- Praise God because he is omnipresent. He is in all places at all times.
- Praise God because he is omnipotent. He is able to do all things.
- Praise God because he is near to us.

Ask- Petition God based on your relationship to him.

- Make requests for needs that are represented among your family members, friends and associates.
- Make requests for needs that you have in your life.
- Commit all your ways and words to God and his plans for your life.

Thanksgiving- Recognize all that God has done for you and thank him.

- List ways that God has provided for your needs and thank him for that.
- Thank God for the people that he has put in your life.
- Remember all the events that God has

orchestrated to work on your behalf and thank him for each one.

- Thank the Lord for specific acts of grace and answers to prayer.

Help- We are nothing without God. Seek his direction and guidance for your life.

- Ask God to inform your decisions and to give you wisdom.
- Look for God's will for you life and for your future.
- Commit all your decisions to his lordship and counsel.

The Lord's Prayer (Matthew 6.9-13)

Jesus taught his disciples- and all believers who were to
follow- to pray. He offered them what we refer to as 'The
Lord's Prayer.' This prayer is to be used as a model for
prayer. It includes all the elements of what would be a
complete and fulfilling prayer time, leading to an
abundant prayer life. When praying consider using this
prayer as a pattern.

Our Father in heaven, Hallowed be Your name. (v. 9)
Our prayer should begin in an attitude of worship and
with words of worship. Spend a few minutes praising the
Lord as you open your prayer.

Your kingdom come. Your will be done on earth as *it*
is **in heaven. (v. 10)** There are two important things to
focus on in this part of your prayer. First of all, come to
God in an attitude of humility. It is his work and will that
we are praying for. Secondly, recognize the sovereignty
of God. He is the ultimate authority in all situations. We
must submit ourselves to his work.

Give us this day our daily bread. (v. 11) We should
realize that all our provision and blessing comes from
God. It is to him that we are to address our requests.
Look to the Lord to meet your needs.

**And forgive us our debts, as we forgive our debtors.
(v. 12)** We can turn to God for the forgiveness of our
sins. As we repent we can be sure of his grace and mercy
in our lives. Additionally, we are to forgive others. This

is not necessarily a requirement for forgiveness, but we must learn to be gracious and forgiving to others.

And do not lead us into temptation, but deliver us from the evil one. (v. 13) There are decisions that we are faced with every day. We should always ask God to guide us toward those positions that will keep us in God's will. Avoid temptation whenever possible and pray for God's protection and leading.

For Yours is the kingdom and the power and the glory forever. Amen. (v. 13) The Lord's Prayer begins with worship. It also ends with worship. Honor God for his eternal power and glory.

Praying the Scriptures
Ephesians 1.15-19

As you spend more time praying and studying the Bible, you will recognize that there is a great convergence in the two things. One of the blessings of the spiritual life for Christians is when we combine our prayers and our Bible study. The Scriptures come alive when they are transformed into prayers. There are many verses, passages and even whole chapters that lend themselves to prayer. Find the ones that work best for you and learn to pray the Word of God.

As an example, begin to pray the following passage for people in your life. This Scripture begins with an introductory comment:

Therefore I also, after I heard of your faith in the Lord Jesus and your love for all the saints, do not cease to give thanks for you, making mention of you in my prayers...

For the remainder of the prayer, substitute the name of the person for whom you are praying wherever the verse says 'you.' For example, you would pray that God would "give to Bob the spirit of wisdom and revelation..."

...that the God of our Lord Jesus Christ, the Father of glory, may give to you the spirit of wisdom and revelation in the knowledge of Him, the eyes of your understanding being enlightened; that you may know what is the hope of His calling, what are the riches of the

glory of His inheritance in the saints, and what is the
exceeding greatness of His power toward us who
believe, according to the working of His mighty power.

You may want to play with the grammar a little bit to fit
your own personality, but the content of the Bible makes
a powerful prayer resource.

Prayer Triplets

Prayer Triplets are a tried and true way to work toward doing evangelism, while at the same time developing your personal prayer life and working toward Christian fellowship and accountability.

- Prayer Triplets require three prayer partners. The prayer partners covenant together to meet regularly (the more frequently the partners meet, the more effective they will be). During their meeting time these prayer partners share concerns with one another, pray for each other and develop a list of others to pray for.

- Each prayer partner will bring the names of three people to the other prayer partners.

  - Pray for one person who needs to be saved.
  - Pray for one person who needs to be healed.
  - Pray for one person who needs peace, strength or direction.

The prayer partners make a commitment to one another to pray for each other and the individuals on each prayer triplet list. Ultimately, each member of the group will pray for eleven people each day: three people who need to be saved, three who are in need of healing, three who need a different touch from God and the two other members of the group.

The Romans Road
An Evangelistic Plan

The Romans Road is a convenient way to remember and share the gospel message with those who do not know Christ. The fundamental outline is all found in the book of Romans from the New Testament. Memorize these verses and practice presenting the gospel in your own words so that you will be prepared to give a witness to those who need to know Jesus.

1. Every person is a sinner and needs to know God.

   All have sinned and fall short of the glory of God. **Romans 3.23**

   There is none righteous, no, not one. **Romans 3.10**

2. There is a punishment for sin separation from God and death.

   For the wages of sin is death. **Romans 6.23**

3. God has an answer to the consequences of sin- life.

   But the gift of God is eternal life in Christ Jesus our Lord. **Romans 6.23**

4. We don't have to be holy to turn to God. He took the initiative and did the work for us.

God demonstrates His own love toward us, in that while we were still sinners, Christ died for us. **Romans 5.8**

5. The way to experience salvation through Christ is to call out to him.

    Whoever calls on the name of the Lord shall be saved. **Romans 10.13**

6. Believing in Christ and telling someone are essential.

    If you confess with your mouth the Lord Jesus and believe in your heart that God has raised Him from the dead, you will be saved. **Romans 10.9**

The John 3.16 Evangelism Model

Based on John 3.16, this is a simple, biblical way to share the gospel with others. The outline of the verse becomes the outline of your gospel presentation. Be sure that you can quote the Scripture passage accurately, but develop your own 'script' to share with others.

For God so loved the world that He gave His only begotten Son,
that whoever believes in Him should not perish but have everlasting life. ***John 3.16***

1. **God loves.** God loves all people. There is no one who is beyond God's grace or outside of his love. Everyone is included in the love of God, and anyone can experience it.

   God so loved the world...

2. **God gives.** It is the nature of the Lord to give gifts to his children. There are no strings on these gifts. He offers them without condition or obligation.

   ...He gave His only begotten Son...

3. **We believe.** The only requirement for the Christian is to believe in God. There is nothing we can do to earn the grace of God, we only have to receive it in faith.

...whoever believes in Him should not perish...

4. **<u>We live.</u>** The result of believing in Christ and receiving the gift of God is life. To be sure of your eternal salvation, learn John 3.16.

   ...whoever believes in Him should not perish but have everlasting life.

God loves.
God gives.
We believe.
We live.

ABC Bible Study

Use the alphabet to guide you as you study the Bible.
This will help you remember important aspects of study.
In addition, you will be sure that you get a well-rounded
look at each passage that you are working on.

A-   A Title
   Jot down two or three titles that come to mind as
you study the passage, then select the   best one, or
make a composite of them. The title should give a
summary of the passage.

B-   Basic Passage
   Choose the verse, or group of verses, which
includes the central meaning or message of passage.
This should include clues to contents of the entire
passage. The passage should show an obvious
connection to the title that you chose in **A.**

C-   Challenge
   As you study the passage, ask God to challenge
your heart in a personal way from the   Scriptures.
As God reveals this to you, write out- in your own
words- the verses that have   especially challenged you.
Then, write out how the verses have challenged you and
what   you plan to do about the challenge.

D-   Difficulties
   Make a note of any verses that raise questions for
you as you read. Write out questions that   you have,
and work toward researching and learning the answers to

your difficulties.

E-   Essence

Write out your own summary of the passage. Try to keep your summary balanced with all   the parts of the passage. One way to do this would be to paraphrase the passage in your   own words.

ABC Bible Study Worksheet

Date _____

Study Passage _____

A Title

_____

Basic Passage

_____

_____

Challenge

_____

_____

     Verse of the Challenge

_____

_____

     Truth of the Challenge

_____

_____

     Personal Application of the Challenge

_____

_____

_____

Difficulties

       Verse   Difficulties

_____

_____

_____

Essence (summary)

_____

_____

_____

Why Study the Bible?

To share it with others
Colossians 3.16 tells us that a very important element of Bible study is to share it with others, believers and non-believers.

To learn about Christ
Romans 15.3-4 shows that a very good reason to study the Bible is to learn about our Lord.

To be comforted
Reading the Bible also helps us in times of grief, stress, discouragement of loneliness. We should be reminded that we need to look for comfort and patience in God's word. (Psalm 119.52)

To be approved by God
By studying the Bible we gain knowledge of God himself. And in doing that we are assured of his approval and grace in our lives. (2 Timothy 2.15)

How to Study the Bible (Psalm 119)

It can be intimidating to read the Bible. There are parts of it that seem archaic and hard to understand, and trying to take in the whole thing is overwhelming, especially if you are not very familiar with reading Scripture. Consider the following tips, all taken from Psalm 119, when reading the Bible.

Psalm 119

- Study all of God's Word. v. 6
- Read the Bible with your whole heart. v. 10
- Memorize Scriptures. v. 11
- Meditate on God's Word. v. 15
- Enjoy reading the Bible. v. 16
- Encounter the Scriptures with an open mind. v. 18
- Apply biblical precepts to your life. v. 24
- Internalize God's word. v. 31
- Study the Bible consistently. v. 33
- Read the Bible in faith. v. 42
- Sing God's word back to him. v. 54
- Study the Bible without procrastinating. v. 60
- Pray the Scriptures. v. 76
- Believe what the Bible has to say. V. 89
- Love God's word. v. 97
- Let the Bible enlighten you. v. 105

Journaling Guidelines

Using a spiritual journal can be a great asset to your spiritual life. By writing regularly you create a record of your own heart, your quest for God and his work in your life. It is not hard to keep a journal and it is impossible to do it 'wrong.' There are no rules or expectations. The spiritual journal is the fruit of a pilgrim, a personal item that can become precious to the Lord, and to the one who follows him.

Although there are no rules, there are some guidelines that might help you get started and to stay focused.

- Get started. As with any spiritual activity, the most important thing is to do it. Do not spend too much time thinking about how to do it, or collecting materials and resources. Start writing today.
- Don't make too big of a deal out of journaling. It is for your benefit and for your eyes only. Don't be concerned about what someone else might think about your reflections. They will never know about them.
- You may be tempted to buy a special journal or blank book for this project. That is unnecessary. Any notebook of any size will work nicely.
- Write your prayers. This could take the form of a letter to God, a conversation or a monologue. Write from your heart.
- Don't worry about not writing enough. Try limiting yourself to something that is

manageable. For example, you may want to write only one page each day.

- Write reflections on what you have learned as you have been reading and studying the Bible.
- You can list prayer requests that you have. Churches and other groups keep lists of parishioners who need prayer. You also can include friends and family members in need.
- If you are praying- and particularly, if you are listing prayer requests- be sure to keep track of answers to prayer.
- You may want to copy in your journal passages of Scripture that are meaningful to you.
- A journal is a great place to keep track of sermon and Bible study notes.
- Use your journal to write favorite Bible verses in your own words. Paraphrasing in this way can help the Scriptures come alive for you.

The Four "I"s Visit

1. **Introduce**
Say, "I am _____ from
_____ Church. I am out
meeting people today so that I can get to know you
better and to see if there is any way that I can serve you."
- *Be as friendly as you can be.*
- *Smile.*
- *Do not be threatening or judgmental.*

2. **Inquire**
Say, "One of the things that we are trying to do is serve
our neighbors. Is there anything that we can do for you?
Do you need anything? Could I pray for you?"
- *Your attitude should be to serve others. We want to
give to them. We are not concerned about what they
can do for us.*
- *Ask a lot of questions and listen. What people say to
you is more important than what you say to them.*
- *Keep accurate records about each visit. This will
help us to know where and how to follow-up with
people.*

3. **Invite**
Say, "We would like to invite you to attend worship with
us. We meet each week at _____(time and place).
It would be great to have you join us. Could we pick you
up next Sunday?"
- *We are inviting people to church, but that is not the
purpose of our visit.*

- *Encourage those who attend worship at another church. We are not trying to convince them to leave their church.*
- *Leave a note or invitation card whether someone is home or not.*

4. **Intercede**

Say, "Would it be alright if I pray for you right now? I want you to know that I care about you and your needs. I will be praying for you all week."

- *You may be uncomfortable praying for people in person. Do it anyway, if you can. If you cannot promise that you will pray for them later. (If you promise to pray later, do it.)*
- *Pray before you leave the door, whether anyone opens or not.*

Starting a Faith Team

Every believer in Christ should be sharing his faith, doing the work of evangelism and looking for opportunities to reach others with the gospel. Some individuals will be called to begin a 'faith team,' a 'community of faith' or a church. The following steps should help you as you begin the work of developing a 'Faith Team.'

- Ask God to arrange things for your faith team. Pray that he will send people who will help you in building up the body of Christ. Pray that you will be led to those who need to hear the gospel and come to faith.

- Begin to be intentional about building relationships and working toward establishing your faith team. Put yourself in places where there are unbelievers. Get acquainted with new people.

- Gather with your team at a non-threatening place. You can meet in a home, park, office, school, restaurant, coffee shop, etc. Find a time and place that will not be offensive, uncomfortable or impractical for any of your faith team members.

- Be a 'church' from the very beginning. You may never think of your faith team as a 'church,' but you should act like one. Make note of the Elements of a Faith Team/ Church.

- Continue to pray for encounters with God. Ask God to continue sending people to you, and to send you to people who are in need. Remember to keep networking all the time.

- Plan and pray for leaders to be raised up from your faith team. You should always be thinking about who will lead the next faith team. Identify those in your group whom God is calling to lead another faith team in the future.

Elements of a Faith Team/ Church

There are certain characteristics that every church (and every Christian for that matter) must manifest. Without these characteristics, or elements, the church will not be able to reach its full potential, or fulfill the will of God. Every Christian needs to mindful of these things and work to put them into practice in his own life and advocate for their presence in the life of the church/ faith team. As a result of diligent- even disciplined- practice, we can expect both spiritual and numerical growth as the Lord draws people to himself.

Bible Study- Every group needs to be built upon the foundation of God's word, the Bible. There should be attention paid to regular reading of the Scriptures as well as study times, interpretations and explanations. Teachings and sermons should be firmly based on what the Bible is saying to the followers of God. Application of the Bible to the daily life of the believer is an important part of reading, learning and following the Bible.

Prayer- Nothing is more important than prayer. The Bible is filled with admonitions to pray. As a result, faith teams should be bathed in prayer. Individuals should be praying for their faith team. Faith team members should be praying for one another. There should be time to pray together in regular faith team meetings. Share your needs with one another so that everyone can pray.

Fellowship- Do not minimize the importance of

Christians spending time with one another enjoying being together. It is important that we develop relationships that cause us to be more faithful to God and more devoted to the spiritual life. Fellowship with others encourages accountability, challenge and support. It is not an accident that the church is often pictured as a family. We are to care for other Christians as brothers and sisters in Christ.

Ministry- Every believer in Christ is called to share his faith and work for the Kingdom of God. The faith team is a perfect place for this to take place. Working together we can be more effective in reaching others with the gospel. Together we can visit the sick and imprisoned. Through the work of Christ we can pray for the healing of the sick. We can preach freedom to those in spiritual bondage, clothe the naked and feed the hungry.

Accountability and Discipleship Questions

Use the following questions in your faith team meetings to encourage discussion, growth in faith and unity in the group.

- Have you been a testimony to Christ this week? How?

- What has been your biggest struggle in the last week?

- What Scriptures have spoken to your soul this week?

- Are you spending time with God in prayer? How is it going? If you have not been praying, why not?

- How have you shared your faith with others? Who are you sharing your faith with?

- In what areas do you need prayer?

- What passage of Scripture have you committed to memory?

Faith Team Agenda
(Sample Meeting)

Suggested guidelines for a faith team meeting/ worship service:

One Hour Meeting:

Fellowship (15 minutes): Begin your meeting by spending some time enjoying being together. Casual introductions, sharing events, upcoming announcements and reports. Toward the end of your fellowship time you should include some of the discipleship and accountability questions for challenging one another and moving into the next segment.

Bible Study (15 minutes): Someone in the group- usually the group leader- will lead in a time of Bible study and exhortation. This can be in the form of a discussion- based study, a lecture or sermonic exhortation, or simply a reading of the Bible together.

Prayer (15 minutes): Share concerns, needs and answers to prayer with one another and then pray together for the group. Silent prayer, unison prayer and prayers led by different members of your group are all good ways to have a meaningful prayer time.

Ministry (15 minutes): This section of the worship/ meeting should flow naturally from the prayer time. Minister to one another with prayer, laying on of hands, counseling, encouragement and strength. You can also spend time brainstorming, planning and executing other outreach ministry programs and events.

90 Minute Meeting:

To extend your meeting for an additional 30 minutes consider some of the following adjustments:

- Include some snacks or refreshments, or even a full meal to be included in your fellowship time.
- Spend more time in prayer. Have different people pray for individual needs.
- Include outreach ministry in your prayer time.
- Extend your Bible time by including a more in depth study followed by discussion.
- Use your accountability questions during fellowship time to lead into opportunities to share testimonies of the work of God.

Kuandaa

Church Planting Resources

Kuandaa Church Planting Covenant

In light of the mission to evangelize the world, and in consideration of Kuandaa International's commitment to train pastors and plant churches, we offer the following proposal. Each church planter/ pastor will be asked to agree to the following covenant with the leadership of Kuandaa International anticipating the presence and blessing of God.

Kuandaa commits to:

- Prayer support for each pastor and congregation

- A mentoring relationship with each pastor

- Unlimited access to all Kuandaa materials

- Weekly communications with Kuandaa mentors (when possible)

- Regular support and advice in ministry matters

- Limited financial support when possible and appropriate

- Kick-off worship service support and cooperation

- Visits and training from Kuandaa International leadership teams

The Pastor/Planter agrees to:

- Scout and identify a location for the new congregation

- Develop a plan for the new church

  o When will worship occur?

  o How will we invite people?

  o Where do we meet?

- Attend all Kuandaa training events

- Attend Kuandaa pastor/planter events

- Maintain regular and meaningful communication with Kuandaa leadership in Uganda and the US

- Maintain accountability in all moral, financial and church-related matters

- Demonstrate a commitment to and progress toward

  o Outreach events

  o Spiritual growth

  o Healthy church practices

  o Educational and Theological pursuits

Kuandaa Affiliation

Support (US) Opportunities

- Sustaining Organization/ Individual-

    ○ Maintains an accountability relationship with Kuandaa and its leaders.

    ○ Supports the mission and work of Kuandaa through prayer, finances and participating in mission opportunities.

- Partner Organizations-

    ○ Support a Member church or new church start by providing internet service for the Member Church pastor.

    ○ Offers scholarships for Member Church pastor and / or leaders.

    ○ Engages in a mentoring relationship with Member Church pastor, communicating regularly with him/ her.

    ○ Provides a 10% share of the stipend for the supervising pastor.

Kuandaa (Mission) Options

- Kuandaa Member Churches

    o Pastors and leaders of Kuandaa Churches will attend Kuandaa International training events and summits annually.

    o Each Kuandaa church will submit a monthly report of attendance, membership, activities and needs for the purpose of accountability.

    o Each Kuandaa Church will register annually with Kuandaa International by submitting the Church Registration Form.

    o Pastors and leaders of Kuandaa Churches will be expected to participate in continuing education opportunities and to use Kuandaa International online resources.

    o Kuandaa Member Churches will submit to a Supervising (regional) pastor.

    o Kaundaa Member Churches will work with Kuandaa International Evangelists

    o Kuandaa Member Church Pastors will engage in a mentoring relationship with another pastor from Kuandaa International.

- Each Kuandaa Church will host Kuandaa International leaders for services and other events.

- These churches support the expansion of the Kingdom of God by

  - Training other churches, pastors and ministry leaders

  - Evangelizing the lost

  - Recruiting others to participate with Kuandaa in the ministry of the gospel.

- Associate Organizations/ Individuals-

  - These groups are ministry organizations that are not strictly churches, but who support the work of Kuandaa.

  - These groups participate by attending and supporting training events.

Kuandaa International, Inc.

Church Registration Form

(to be completed annually by October 1)

Church Name _____

Church Address _____

Regular Day and Time of Worship

_____

Name of Pastor _____

Phone Number _____

Facebook Name _____

Have you read, and are you in agreement with the
Kuandaa International affiliation guidelines?
_____ Yes _____ No

Are you willing to make a one year commitment to Kuandaa International?

_____ Yes _____ No

Signature of Pastor

_____

Date _____

Kuandaa International, Inc.

Monthly Church Report Form

Date _____

Church Name

_____

Church Address

_____

Regular Day and Time of Worship

_____

Name of Pastor

_____

Phone Number

_____

Average Attendance at worship service _____

Number of services in the past month _____

Number of people saved this month _____

What are your outreach plans?

_____

_____

_____

_____

What are your church planting plans?

_____

_____

What needs are you currently experiencing?

_____

Signature of Pastor

_____

Date _____